ESTATE PLANNING

HOW TO ORGANIZE YOUR ASSETS, SAVE THOUSANDS IN LEGAL COSTS, CREATE A LIVING TRUST, AND PASS ON YOUR LEGACY WITHOUT LEGAL HEADACHES WITH THIS STEP-BY-STEP PLAN

LUCAS STERLING

TOP TIER PRESS

CONTENTS

INTRODUCTION

Few topics generate more discomfort—and more confusion—than estate planning. For many adults, it conjures images of mahogany offices, stacks of legal documents, and the wealthy brooding over family fortunes. Too often, the question of a will, trust, or power of attorney is quietly pushed aside, dismissed as something to tackle "someday," or assumed unnecessary unless you have vast assets or are approaching retirement. But here's the truth: estate planning isn't just for the rich, the elderly, or those with complicated financial portfolios. It's for everyone who cares about protecting what matters most—your loved ones, your home, your hard-earned savings, and your peace of mind.

If you're reading this, chances are you're not alone in feeling uncertain about where to begin. Maybe you're a parent wanting to ensure your children are cared for if the unthinkable happens. Perhaps you own a home or have started building savings and want to know how to prevent legal headaches for your family down the line. You might be caring for aging parents and are becoming all too aware of the challenges that come when someone passes without a plan. Or perhaps you've witnessed the emotional and financial turmoil left in the wake of a loved one's passing, wishing there had been better preparation. No matter what stage of life you're at, estate planning can help you take control, reduce stress, and leave a positive legacy.

Let's start by busting a persistent myth: estate planning is not reserved for millionaires, retirees, or people with sprawling investment accounts. In reality, most families—middle-income earners, first-time homeowners, single parents, blended families, and even young professionals just starting to build wealth—stand to benefit the most from having a clear plan in place. In fact, the absence of planning can have the greatest impact on people who can least afford unexpected legal costs or prolonged uncertainty.

Consider this: What would happen if something occurred to you tomorrow? Who would make decisions about your health care or finances if you couldn't speak for yourself? How quickly could your loved ones access your accounts or manage your property? Without a legally valid estate plan, the answers to these questions shift away from your family's wishes and into the hands of state laws and courts. The process is called probate—a lengthy and often expensive legal ordeal that can freeze assets, create delays, and impose significant court fees. Even simple cases can stretch on for months, requiring family members to navigate paperwork, hearings, and government bureaucracy at a time when they may already be overwhelmed by grief.

The lack of an estate plan doesn't just create legal obstacles; it can also lead to painful family disputes, lost savings, and irreparable relationships. Imagine siblings arguing over parental possessions, spouses unable to access bank accounts, or caregivers struggling to pay bills or make urgent medical decisions because proper documents weren't in place. These situations aren't rare—they play out in families every single day, regardless of income level or background. Many people don't realize that their "modest" estate, which includes a house, some savings, retirement accounts, and sentimental belongings, still requires careful planning to ensure it reaches the appropriate beneficiaries efficiently and safely.

But this book isn't written to scare you—it's written to empower you. Taking control of your estate plan now is one of the greatest gifts you can give yourself and those you love. Planning ahead provides clarity, saves time and money, and ensures your choices—not a judge's or state government's—determine what happens if life takes an unexpected turn. Having a well-thought-out estate plan provides you with the assurance that your family won't struggle to find solutions in times of need. It allows you to specify guardians for your children, select trusted individuals to handle your affairs, protect vulnerable family members, and pass on your values along with your assets. Even better, getting started is far less daunting than you might think. With the right guidance, clear steps, and modern tools, creating or updating an estate plan can be straightforward and affordable—even if you don't hire an expensive attorney.

This book is your roadmap through the estate planning process, designed specifically for everyday people—not just lawyers or the ultra-wealthy. Whether you're a parent, homeowner, caregiver, retiree, or simply someone who values a secure future, you'll find practical advice tailored to your circumstances. We'll break down complex concepts using plain language and real-world examples, helping you cut through legal jargon and zero in on what actually matters. You'll learn:

- Why every adult should have key documents in place—regardless of age, marital status, or net worth.
- How to set up a simple, cost-effective estate plan that meets your needs and fits your budget.
- Steps for choosing guardians, executors, and decision-makers you trust.
- Strategies to avoid common pitfalls like probate delays, court battles, and unnecessary legal bills.
- Tips on updating your plan as your life evolves, from marriage and parenthood to divorce, second marriages, or changing assets.

- Special considerations for blended families, business owners, and caregivers managing aging parents' estates.
- Ways to communicate your wishes and foster family harmony before and after you're gone.

You may feel overwhelmed or uncertain about where to begin, and that's completely normal. Estate planning often feels unfamiliar, technical, and emotionally charged. The good news? Once you understand the essentials, each step becomes manageable—and the sense of relief you'll feel is well worth the effort. This book will walk you through the process one chapter at a time, offering checklists, explanations, and sample scenarios to guide your decisions.

Remember, estate planning isn't about focusing on worst-case scenarios. It's about proactively shaping the future for yourself and those you care about, ensuring your hard work and values live on. It's about sparing your family needless frustration, saving money that would otherwise go to legal fees, and making sure the things you cherish end up in the right hands. It's about making your voice heard, no matter what tomorrow brings.

No matter your age, relationship status, or financial situation, taking charge of your estate plan is an act of responsibility—and of love. You don't need to be wealthy or ready to retire. You simply need the desire to safeguard your future and look out for the people closest to you. Let's erase the barriers, replace confusion with clarity, and get you on track to building a plan that truly reflects your wishes. The journey starts now.

UNLOCK YOUR ESTATE PLANNING & LIVING TRUST COMPANION WORKBOOK

Ready to turn your estate planning goals into clarity, confidence, and lasting peace of mind?

As a thank-you for reading this book, I've created a helpful companion resource: **The Estate Planning & Living Trust Companion Workbook.** This practical guide helps you organize documents, define your legacy, and create a trust that reflects your values. It's designed to take you from uncertainty to assurance in just a few thoughtful steps.

What's included in this resource:

- Clarify your estate planning goals
- Organize and record key information and assets
- Simplify trust creation and beneficiary planning
- Protect your loved ones and ensure your wishes are honored

👉 **Access Your Companion Workbook**
Visit: **https://content.toptierpress.com/simplify-planning-journey**

Or scan the QR code below to get instant access!

CHAPTER 1

ESTATE PLANNING BASICS – WHAT, WHY, AND WHEN

Estate planning is often misunderstood as something only necessary for the wealthy or elderly, but this belief overlooks its true purpose and broad relevance. Regardless of your age or income, having a clear plan in place ensures that your wishes are respected, your loved ones are cared for, and potential legal complications are minimized. Many people delay these important decisions because the topic feels complicated or intimidating, yet putting off estate planning can lead to confusion and conflict when unexpected events occur.

This chapter breaks down estate planning into simple, understandable terms and explains why it matters to anyone with assets or dependents. It guides you through the key concepts and shows how making thoughtful choices now can save your family time, money, and stress later. By understanding the essentials, you'll gain confidence to take control of your future and the security to protect what matters most.

Understanding Estate Planning & Key Terms

Planning what happens to your property, money, and responsibilities isn't just for the wealthy or the elderly. Estate planning helps you make decisions about how your belongings and care will be managed both during your life and after you pass away. It allows you to protect what matters most, reduce confusion, spare loved ones from difficult choices, and ensure your wishes are clear in advance. For a young parent, this might mean choosing a trusted guardian for their children. For a homeowner, it could involve deciding who will inherit the family house or how any debts will be handled. Even for someone with modest possessions, estate planning lightens the burden on friends and family by giving them clear guidance during a difficult time.

Estate planning includes more than a single document or decision. It brings together several elements that work as one. A central piece is the will. Think of a will as a written set of instructions explaining where your belongings should go, who will care for your children, and who will oversee your plans. For example, if you collect coins and want your nephew to have them, your will ensures that wish is honored. If you have children under eighteen, naming a guardian can prevent family disputes or court involvement later.

Next, there's the trust. Imagine a trust as a locked box holding money or property. You set the rules by deciding who gets the key, who benefits, and when things are given out. With a trust, a parent can make sure a child inherits money only once they reach a certain age, or they can help a family member with disabilities receive support long-term. A trust can also limit taxes and avoid long legal steps for your loved ones.

Estate does not mean a grand mansion. Your estate includes everything you own—your home, car, jewelry, bank accounts, and even pets. If you have a plant collection or a beloved cat, these are part of your estate. Estate planning makes sure each piece ends up where you want.

Probate is the legal process that happens after you die, when your estate is sorted, debts are paid, and what's left goes to the people you selected. This process can take a long time and sometimes costs money. For instance, if you leave a will naming your sister to receive your record collection, probate makes that official. Having a will or trust can shorten or even skip the probate process.

Every plan needs someone to see it through. That's the executor. An executor is like the team captain of your estate, making sure your instructions are followed. If you choose your best friend to be executor, he or she will collect belongings, pay off your bills from your bank account, and hand out your possessions as directed in your will.

A beneficiary is anyone you choose to receive something from your estate. These might be family, friends, charities, or anyone important to you. For example, Anna leaves her childhood books to her niece and a donation to her favorite animal shelter—the niece and the shelter are beneficiaries.

Here's how all these pieces connect. The estate is what you own. The will lists your wishes and names an executor, who's in charge. The executor collects what's in your estate, pays any debts, and gives your belongings to the beneficiaries named in your will. If you have a trust, the person managing it (the trustee) follows your instructions by handing out assets in the time and way that you set. Probate is the system that checks everything that happens legally. Each step helps your loved ones manage the business of loss with fewer complications and less stress.

Being prepared with an estate plan is not about how much money you have or how old you are. It is about helping those you care for when you cannot be there yourself. Creating a plan gives you greater control, saves your family extra trouble, and makes tough times easier to handle. The next step grows from this sense of protection and clarity—knowing when to act and what tools fit your needs the best. This awareness shows why starting sooner can make a difference no matter your age or financial situation, setting the stage for the choices ahead.

Why Estate Planning Matters and When to Start

Clarity about what a will does, or what an executor manages, takes estate planning out of the realm of abstract paperwork and makes its uses feel real. Understanding that a will allows you to designate who inherits the house, and that a power of attorney ensures bills are paid while you're in the hospital, is important for real families. Estate planning is not a task saved for wealthy or older people; it's for anyone with something or someone to protect. Every parent who sets up a guardian for their child, or every homeowner who wants to prevent heirs from fighting over who gets what, uses estate planning tools rooted in those basic terms. A will is just the start of deciding who takes care of your family and what becomes of your home. For those caring for aging parents, documents like powers of attorney help families carry out a loved one's wishes smoothly, sidestepping frustration and confusion.

Some myths stand in the way of prompt and useful estate planning. Many people believe estate planning only applies to those with large bank accounts, vacation homes, or valuable stocks. In fact, if you have a bank account at all, a car, treasured personal possessions, or a story about how a family memento almost got lost after a funeral, estate planning concerns you. Some hold off, reasoning, "I'm too young," or "I'll get to it when I've built up more savings." Yet, life events rarely follow a neat timeline. Illness, accidents, or sudden changes can upend plans at any stage. Imagine a young couple with a new baby—unexpected events could leave a child's care in limbo unless a will names a guardian. Homeowners who wait to spell out who inherits their property may leave families scrambling in probate court, fighting over who owns the house or how it gets divided. Even adult children managing affairs for aging parents sometimes find themselves locked out of accounts or unable to step in when there's no plan on file.

Estate planning gives families a sense of order and security. It shrinks the risk of arguments over property, keeps sensitive health decisions from falling to strangers or the courts, and can keep costs low by helping people avoid long, expensive legal processes. Few things cause more stress in hard times than not knowing what to do or who gets to decide for someone who can no longer speak for themselves. Taking time to make basic choices now gives everyone a firmer footing when unexpected events arrive.

Major life events are the best moments to create or update an estate plan. These include:

- Getting married or entering a partnership
- Getting divorced or separated
- Having a child or adopting
- Buying or selling property, such as a house or land
- Facing a health diagnosis, injury, or major surgery
- Starting or closing a business
- Inheriting money or property from someone else

Your plan should be reviewed, as these changes can alter your possessions or who you protect. A sensible rule is to check your estate plan every few years or when something important shifts in your life. Outdated documents may name incorrect people, leave out new children or grandchildren, or refer to property you no longer own. Keeping your plan up to date helps avoid confusion and gives your family what they need.

Getting started is not as hard as it seems. Begin with a list of everything you own and who you'd want to receive it. Write down things like bank and retirement accounts, your house, a car, jewelry, or personal keepsakes. Make another list of people you trust to handle your affairs if something happens: potential guardians for children, backup decision-makers, or friends who know you well. Gather critical paperwork—property deeds, account statements, insurance policies, titles, and any prior wills or legal agreements. Use a checklist or worksheet to keep things organized and avoid missing important steps.

No one's plan will be perfect on the first try. The best action is to make a start now, putting basic choices on paper and updating them as life goes on. Changes can always be made later as your situation and wishes evolve. This simple, direct approach moves estate planning from something overwhelming to something manageable. By starting early, you give your family clarity, confidence, and protection from avoidable trouble. These first steps help you learn how to manage your estate.

Building Your Foundation: A Clear Recap

A robust estate plan provides comfort to individuals seeking to safeguard their assets and provide for their loved ones. It's not just about who gets what; it's about making your wishes known, handling your assets as you want, and protecting your dependents from confusion or conflict. An estate plan puts you in the driver's seat, giving you a clear say over what happens to your property, finances, and even your personal care when you can no longer make those decisions yourself.

At the center of estate planning is the will, a legal document that lists exactly how your assets—money, property, and possessions—should be given out after you're gone. The will is also where parents can name guardians for minor children, a step that gives lasting security to families in unexpected situations. Without a will, state law decides who gets what, and relatives may face delays and disagreements.

Another central term is trust. A trust is a way to set aside assets so that a trustee, a person or institution you pick, can manage them for a beneficiary. For example, you might set up a trust so your children receive their inheritance at a certain age or for safe management of money for someone with special needs. Trusts help avoid probate, keep financial details private, and offer flexibility in how and when assets are distributed. They can be a smart choice when families want to prevent disputes by spelling out the rules beforehand.

Probate is the court process that happens when someone dies and their will needs to be carried out. Probate gathers the person's assets, pays debts and bills, and makes sure property is passed on according to their wishes as written in the will. This process can take months or even longer, and the costs can eat into the estate. A careful estate plan can help keep probate simple or, in some cases, avoid it altogether.

Every will needs an executor. This is the person who handles the details—filing the will, dealing with debts, paying taxes, and distributing property. The executor is a trusted helper who follows the instructions in your plan. Deciding who should take this role is a major part of making your estate plan work smoothly.

The people or organizations who inherit assets from a will or trust are called beneficiaries. These might be loved ones, friends, or charities. Stating clearly who the beneficiaries are makes your plan clear and avoids hurt feelings or arguments.

Estate planning offers many benefits that reach beyond just distributing money or property. It reduces the chance of family disputes, makes sure minor children and dependents are supported, and gives you the chance to set out medical or financial wishes in case you're no longer able to express them directly. For instance, naming a guardian in your will ensures that children will have a stable home, rather than leaving the decision to courts or relatives who might disagree. Putting property in a trust can give adult children access to funds at a steady pace, which helps avoid wasteful spending or fights among siblings.

The best time to create or update an estate plan isn't limited to one's later years. Any adult who owns assets—or who has children or other people relying on them—needs a plan. Big life moments give you a reason to take action or make changes. Key events that should prompt you to review your plan include:

- Marriage or divorce
- Birth or adoption of a child
- Buying or selling a major asset like a house or business
- Retirement
- Major changes in health, finances, or family relationships

A good estate plan isn't a single event, but an ongoing process that keeps pace with your life. Even if you made a plan years ago, revisiting it after any major change is wise. This way, your wishes—and the well-being of those you care about—stay protected.

Taking action begins with a few clear steps. Listing out what you own, from bank accounts to family heirlooms, gives you a full picture of your estate. Thinking through who you trust most to act as an executor or trustee ensures capable, honest management. Talking with loved ones about your goals turns your wishes into a shared understanding and can prevent confusion when the time comes.

Choosing to handle estate planning now puts you in control. With this knowledge, you can move forward with purpose, clear direction, and the confidence that your wishes—and those you love—are well cared for.

Main Points Recap

Now that you understand the key elements of estate planning and why it matters for people at every stage of life, you can take confident steps toward securing your future and protecting those you care about most. By starting early and keeping your plan current, you reduce stress, avoid unnecessary legal hurdles, and give your family clear instructions when they need them most. Whether you're safeguarding a home, naming guardians for children, or ensuring your wishes are honored, this knowledge empowers you to make thoughtful choices with clarity and control. Moving forward, use these insights as a foundation to build or update your estate plan—transforming what once seemed complex into a manageable process that offers peace of mind today and tomorrow.

CHAPTER 2
TAKING INVENTORY – WHAT YOU OWN AND WHAT YOU OWE

More than half of Americans don't have a clear list of their assets and debts when it comes time to plan their estate. This lack of organization can lead to confusion, delays, and unexpected costs for families trying to settle affairs during difficult times. Without a clear picture of what you own and what you owe, even simple tasks like paying bills or transferring property can become complicated and stressful for those left behind. By taking the initial step to inventory your financial life, you can gain control and clarity, which in turn lays the foundation for seamless planning and peace of mind. This chapter begins that essential process—helping you create a straightforward map of your financial world so you and your loved ones avoid unnecessary challenges down the road.

Cataloging Your Assets and Liabilities

Breaking your financial world into assets and liabilities gives you a clear starting point for estate planning. This approach provides real control over your affairs and ensures that nothing is overlooked. Take out a notebook and create two pages: one labeled **"What You Own"** and the other **"What You Owe."** The more accurate and organized your records are now, the fewer complications your loved ones will face later.

Begin with assets. List everything you own that has value, grouping items by category. The most straightforward assets are your bank and savings accounts. Record the name of each bank, the type of account (checking, savings, certificate of deposit), the account holder's name, and an approximate balance. If you share an account with a spouse, parent, or someone else, note whether it's **joint** or **individual.** For example: *John and Lisa – Checking account, First State Bank, Joint, $3,200.*

Next, move to retirement savings. Include IRAs, 401(k)s, company pensions, and similar plans. Note which accounts you own individually and which are shared. Record the financial institution and estimate the current value. For example: *Lisa's 401(k), Widget Corp, Individual owner, $86,000.* These accounts are often among the most valuable parts of an estate, so accuracy is essential.

Include brokerage and investment accounts, even if the balance is small. Every asset counts. For each account, record the brokerage name, the type of account, owner, and the present value: "John, personal brokerage account, Main Street Investments, $14,500." Also note life insurance policies, especially if they have a cash value. For policies like whole life or universal life, list the insurer, type of policy, name(s) of owner and insured, and cash value if any: "Lisa, whole life policy, Sunny Life Insurance, owner and insured, $12,000 cash value."

Real estate requires its grouping. Detail every property, even vacation cabins, rental homes, or empty land lots. State the address, description, approximate market value, and who owns it: "123 Maple Ave, primary residence, market value $400,000, owned jointly by John and Lisa." For timeshares or land parcels, mention the property type, company, and location: "Bear Valley Timeshare, Mountain Resorts, Lisa, $4,000 value."

Next, turn to vehicles. Count each car, truck, motorcycle, recreational vehicle, or boat, with model, year, and an estimated value: "John, 1968 Ford Mustang, classic car, individually owned, appraised at $10,000." Remember to include trailers, ATVs, and other vehicles if they have worth.

Round out assets with significant personal property. Think about jewelry, family heirlooms, antiques, collectibles, valuable electronics, musical instruments, artwork, or any special collections. Each item needs a brief description and estimated worth: "Lisa, diamond engagement ring, $2,500 estimated value." Grouping these things makes it easier to see where your most sentimental or valuable non-cash property lives.

Be as thorough and honest as possible. Missed items can cause disputes or confusion later. Even small retirement accounts or a piece of inherited jewelry should go on the list. If you're not sure of the value, use your best guess for now and adjust in the future.

After organizing your assets, move onto liabilities. Write down all debts and obligations still attached to you or shared with others. Start with home mortgages and lines of credit. For each, give the property address tied to the debt, name of lender, balance owed, and payment terms if you know them: "Home mortgage, 123 Maple Ave, National Home Lenders, $150,000 remaining, 30-year fixed, joint."

Car loans and other vehicle payments follow, each with the lender's name, vehicle description, amount owed, and loan term: "Car loan, 2019 Honda CR-V, Lisa, First Union Bank, $10,000 outstanding, five-year term." Don't forget student loans, medical bills, credit cards, and personal or business loans. Each entry should mirror the same level of detail: "Federal student loan, Lisa, $25,000 balance, U.S. Department of Education," "Credit card, John, Capital Plus, $2,500 balance, minimum due $60/month."

Group all debts together by type—real estate, auto, student, consumer credit—so you spot gaps or risks in your planning. This structure lays out both your obligations and the present strengths, making next steps easier.

Don't worry if values or balances aren't perfect. Write what you know, then update as you gather new information. The goal at this stage is to see your whole financial world at a glance. Having a well-sorted inventory means fast, smooth preparation for documentation.

Start gathering account statements, appraisals, and digital copies of titles or policies. These will support your records, make updates simple, and prove ownership and debts as you head deeper into estate planning.

Documenting Your Financial Information Clearly

Creating a thorough record-keeping system is one of the most valuable steps you can take after assembling your list of what you own and owe. Turning your inventory into an organized, easy-to-find record shifts it from a simple list to a tool that supports real protection and flexibility for yourself and your family. Well-documented records form the backbone of any estate plan. They remove confusion, prevent missed steps, and allow you and others to respond efficiently during yearly reviews or unexpected events.

Choosing your method of documentation depends on your comfort, privacy needs, and habits. People who prefer handwriting may use a dedicated notebook or a set of labeled folders. Digital users often choose spreadsheets, secure cloud documents, or estate planning software. Each format works as long as you commit to using it consistently and updating it as your life changes.

For each asset or debt, add accurate details that make your record truly useful. Start with the name of the item—for example, "ABC Bank Checking Account" or "Main Street Home Mortgage." Incorporate account or identification numbers, the full address of a property, or the VIN for a vehicle. Include who owns the asset—yours alone, shared with a spouse, or held in trust. Note how the account is titled, since this affects how the asset transfers. List the location of important papers, deed originals, or safe deposit keys.

Contact details are vital. Record the phone number or email for a bank, investment firm, or insurance company, along with a specific representative if possible. If an asset has an online login, document the username (avoiding passwords in open records) along with where and how login credentials are stored securely. When dealing with debts, list the lender's contact information, current terms, payment method, and the location of documents or online access points.

A repeatable structure makes the process simpler and helps you spot what is missing. Here's an approach for physical records:

- Use a set of folders divided by asset type (bank accounts, retirement, property, vehicles, life insurance, debts)
- Label each folder clearly with both content type and owner
- Place supporting documents (bank statements, deeds, titles, insurance certificates) in the correct folder
- Store the folders in a secure location like a locked drawer or safe

For digital records, mirror this system:

- Create a folder on your computer or a secure drive for each asset type
- Use consistent file names such as "2024 IRA Statement – ABC Investments" or "Car Loan Agreement – City Credit Union"
- Save digital scans or PDFs of physical records with clear descriptions
- Back up files on password-protected USB drives or secure cloud storage
- For extra assurance, keep a written guide or "map" of the folder system, indicating where key documents are saved and how to access them

A basic spreadsheet can become a powerful tool for tracking. List columns for asset type, account number, owner, institution, contact name, location of documents, date last checked, and special notes. Estate planning software often prompts for these details, and you can choose a program that fits your comfort with technology.

Regular review keeps your data accurate. Place a reminder in your calendar to check your inventory each year, as soon as you receive new account statements or after a big event like refinancing your mortgage or selling property. Use a checklist at the front of your documentation binder or digital folder to track the last update, who signed off, and when next to review. This habit prevents overlooked accounts or outdated addresses.

Here's a clear example of the difference organization makes:

Vague record: "Retirement accounts at XYZ Bank"

Actionable record:

- Asset: Roth IRA
- Institution: XYZ Bank
- Account number: 349021
- Owner: Joint (me and spouse)
- Branch contact: Andrea Lee, 555-9876
- Last statement location: Digital folder "Retirement/2024 Roth IRA"
- Online access: Username in password manager

Storing sensitive details safely matters as much as recording them. Never include passwords in plain view or unsecured files. For digital stores, use encrypted, password-protected documents and keep backup copies offline. Dedicated USB drives, locked file drawers, or secure home safes offer strong protection for physical documents.

Thorough documentation isn't just a personal shield; it's a gift to anyone who may need to act on your behalf someday. Detailed records save loved ones from confusion, delays, and stress during vital moments. Organizing now makes updates, sharing, and future transitions more manageable for all parties involved. Careful records pave the way for legal and family needs, ensuring all your work and planning truly count when they are most needed.

The Importance for Heirs and Legal Purposes

Putting together a detailed inventory of what you own and what you owe forms the backbone of any solid estate plan. Doing this helps your family and legal representatives avoid confusion or arguments later. When you leave behind a well-organized record of your finances, you save your heirs from long searches for missing documents, surprise debts, or heated debates over who should get what. For example, an updated list of your bank accounts, retirement plans, and real estate can turn a complicated legal process into a straightforward one. Your executor will have a clear roadmap to follow, letting them act quickly to pay off debts and distribute your property according to your wishes. Without this, your loved ones might spend months searching for accounts or struggle to pay final bills, all while dealing with grief.

Why Clear Inventories Make Things Easier

A full, up-to-date financial inventory isn't only for the wealthy. Every family, regardless of income or total assets, benefits from having this record. Imagine two siblings dealing with their parent's estate. If everything is spelled out on paper—even the details about an old car loan or a small insurance policy—there is less chance for resentment or suspicion. A clear inventory means no one needs to guess at your intentions or hunt for clues about what you owned. This reduces the risk of arguments or even legal contests.

Documentation can also protect against outside errors. Sometimes, banks freeze accounts because no one can immediately prove who should access them. If you leave behind a clear, legally accepted record that outlines your accounts, your executor can respond to questions with confidence and speed. This means your bills get paid on time, and your family isn't left waiting for funds they may urgently need for things like funeral costs or home expenses.

Legal Compliance and Avoiding Pitfalls

Estate laws require accurate reporting of all assets and debts. State and federal regulations often call for detailed lists that include property values, retirement accounts, cash, loans, and valuables such as jewelry or collectibles. Preparing these records in advance helps your executor save time and reduce legal costs, avoiding the need for professional asset searches. Some states even impose penalties on estates that fail to make timely or accurate disclosures, which can drain resources intended for your heirs.

If these requirements aren't met, the consequences can include expensive delays or, in serious cases, lawsuits. For example, if your plan omits several credit card debts and an overseas investment account, your executor might miss essential payments, resulting in added interest charges or legal claims against the estate. In addition, an incomplete or inaccurate inventory can give dissatisfied relatives grounds to challenge your will or dispute ownership of your assets. Courts may then freeze accounts or launch lengthy investigations, leaving your family in uncertainty until everything is resolved.

Peace of Mind for You and Your Loved Ones

Knowing that every detail is in place gives comfort both to you and to your loved ones. A thorough inventory becomes a living document. Life changes are easier to handle because you can update your record when you buy a new house, switch banks, split a retirement account in divorce, or change insurance beneficiaries. You're not stuck starting from scratch during a crisis or major life event.

Many people think listing their assets is too big a job or that only wealthy families benefit from these efforts. The truth is that families with modest means may face even greater challenges if there's confusion about bills or property. For example, if you leave a small life insurance policy but no one knows about it, your family may never claim the money you intended for them. Or, if you pass down a house but don't record unpaid property taxes, your heirs may inherit an unexpected cost.

Typical Assets and Liabilities to Include

Your inventory should cover:

Assets

- Checking and savings accounts
- Investment and retirement plans
- Real estate (homes, land)
- Vehicles
- Life insurance policies
- Personal property (valuables, jewelry, collectibles)

Liabilities

- Mortgages and home equity loans
- Credit card balances
- Car loans
- Personal loans

Including these means less chance your estate misses a payment or fails to secure a benefit. Bank accounts close properly, and old debts don't surprise heirs. Every step that you take to clarify these things now makes life easier for those you care about, lightening the emotional and practical burdens that can follow a loss. This sense of order and preparation gives you real peace of mind while offering clear support to those you may leave behind.

Bringing It All Together

Now that you clearly understand how to organize and document your assets and liabilities, you are ready to take the crucial next step in estate planning with confidence. By creating a detailed and well-maintained financial inventory, you lay the foundation for protecting your family's future, simplifying legal processes, and minimizing costs. This preparation not only reduces stress for your loved ones but also ensures your wishes are respected and followed smoothly when the time comes. Moving forward, keep your records updated regularly so that your estate plan remains accurate and effective, giving you peace of mind today and security for tomorrow.

CHAPTER 3

UNDERSTANDING WILLS – YOUR FIRST LINE OF CONTROL

More than half of adults in the United States pass away without leaving a valid will, leaving their families to face lengthy legal processes, unexpected expenses, and decisions made by courts rather than loved ones. When someone dies without clear instructions, state laws step in to divide property according to fixed rules that may not reflect personal wishes or family dynamics. Without this crucial document, even simple belongings can become sources of confusion and conflict among those left behind. Understanding how a will functions is the first step toward ensuring your intentions are honored, your assets protected, and your family shielded from unnecessary hardship.

What a Will Covers—and What Happens Without One

A will is a legal document that explains what should happen to your belongings after you pass away. If you own a house, a car, bank accounts, or items with personal meaning, your will specifies who should receive them. Many people imagine a will as something only the wealthy need, but in reality, it's useful for anyone who wants control over their home, cherished possessions, savings, or plans for their children's care.

A will applies to assets owned solely in your name. These might include a family home titled only to you, a car you purchased, your checking account, or a box of treasured letters stored in your attic. For example, if a parent owns a house and wants both children to inherit it equally, that wish can be stated clearly in the will. They might also leave jewelry to a sister or a vintage record collection to a close friend. All of this works only when the assets are owned by that individual alone and not shared with another person.

Some assets live outside a will's reach, regardless of what you write. Jointly owned assets, like a house co-owned with a spouse, skip the will entirely. These pass directly to the surviving owner by law. Retirement accounts, life insurance policies, and certain bank accounts have their own "beneficiary" forms. This means if you listed your nephew as your IRA beneficiary, even if your will says something else, that account will still go to your nephew. The same is true for property or accounts held in trust—you cannot change those directions with a will. These exceptions can surprise families who didn't realize the will's instructions only apply to certain types of property.

Let's look at a real-life example. Imagine Helen, a widowed mother, writes a will leaving her home to her daughter and her savings to her son. Her car, owned jointly with her son, does not appear in the will because it transfers to him directly. Her old life insurance policy, naming her friend as beneficiary, goes to the friend, even though the will states all assets go to her children. Because she only owned the family home in her name, her daughter receives it according to the will.

There are common misunderstandings about a will's powers. Some families guess a will can override beneficiary names on insurance or make changes to property already in trust, but it cannot. A will cannot direct who gets assets you have already promised elsewhere; it works only with property you own outright that doesn't have its instructions. Any plans involving family trusts, joint accounts, or designated insurance payments need separate legal work.

A will does not put conditions on how money is spent after you die unless you use specialized tools—like a trust within a will, which takes more legal steps. You cannot prevent someone from selling a house or mandate that the proceeds be spent in a specific manner using only an ordinary will. These situations require additional planning and should not rely solely on simple will language.

When a person dies without a valid will, their estate is considered "intestate." In this case, state inheritance laws take over and dictate who gets what. The court appoints an administrator—often the closest living relative—to manage everything. The result often surprises families. The process takes more time. There are extra court fees, plus the administrator has to account for every step, making things slower and sometimes more costly. The court divides property between close relatives in a set order, regardless of any emotional connections or verbal promises.

For example, when a mother dies without a will, her estate usually divides equally between her two adult children. But if she lived most of her life with a long-term partner, that person may receive nothing. If there are minor children, the court steps in and decides on a guardian, which may not be the person the parent wanted. Blended families face new problems: a stepchild raised as a daughter will not inherit unless named in a will. Unmarried partners, friends, or charities the person cared about all risk receiving nothing, since state law does not recognize informal promises or non-relatives.

These situations create hurt feelings, extra expenses, and sometimes long court fights. There is also a loss of privacy, since the probate process becomes a matter of public record. Family members might be left with a pile of paperwork just to claim the simplest things, like jewelry or household items.

To gain control and bring clarity, a person needs a legally valid will. That means putting wishes in writing, signing the document, and having witnesses watch and confirm the signing, as local law requires. Including every type of property, even digital or sentimental items, helps carry out the writer's true intentions. With this groundwork in place, anyone can begin to build a reliable will that protects their loved ones and reduces future uncertainty.

Steps to Writing a Legally Valid Will

Having a clear understanding of what a will can and cannot do prioritizes the next step: putting those wishes into writing in a manner recognized by the law. For your will to achieve its purpose after you pass away, every detail must line up with foundational legal standards. The foundation begins with comprehending the legal rules that provide a will with its validity.

Legal Requirements: Laying the Groundwork

A valid will starts with a testator, who must have the capacity to make one. Most places require the testator to be at least 18 years old. Mental capacity is just as critical. The law expects you to know the meaning of a will, be able to identify your property, and recognize the people you wish to benefit. Anyone struggling with serious confusion or under the control of someone else risks having their will thrown out.

Wills must be written, typed or handwritten. A will that is spoken out loud or written on a napkin does not count as valid. The document needs to show a "statement of testamentary intent," meaning it must plainly declare this is your will. "I declare this to be my Last Will and Testament" is a powerful sentence that makes a significant impact.

Witnesses and Signatures: Locking in Validity

Signing the will correctly is a central step. You, as the testator, must sign at the end of the will. If you can't sign, most places allow someone to sign for you in your presence and by your direction, but only if you're mentally able.

Witnesses are just as important as your signature. Most places require at least two, sometimes three, adults who don't stand to gain from your will. These witnesses must be "disinterested," meaning none can be an heir or beneficiary. Using a beneficiary as a witness is one of the most common blunders. Doing this can void gifts to that person or, in some cases, the entire will.

The process for witnessing usually looks like this:

1. Bring together your chosen witnesses.
2. Sign your will in front of them, or acknowledge a prior signature as your own.
3. Ask each witness to sign the will in your presence and in each other's presence.

Each jurisdiction has its quirks, but sticking to these broad points covers the basics.

Language and Clarity: Precision Over Guesswork

Wording is everything in a will. The best wills use clear, plain words to leave no room for different interpretations. If your will says, "I leave my personal items as my family needs," you risk sparking fights. The courts struggle to decide who counts as "family" and what you meant by "as my family needs." Better wording would be, "I leave my jewelry, listed on Schedule A, to my niece, Olivia Jones."

Here are some phrases that courts welcome:

- "I give my home at 123 Maple Lane, including all contents, to my son, Alex Lee."
- "My 2017 Toyota Camry goes to my daughter, Jasmine Doe."
- "My savings account at First City Bank, account number ending in 9287, will be divided equally between my grandchildren."

Problem phrases that spark family fights and court cases:

- "I leave my car to my child." (Which child? What if you have more than one?)
- "Divide my estate fairly." (What does "fairly" mean in dollars or items?)

Pay close attention to details that matter, such as names, addresses, or details about special items. The tighter the wording, the lower the chance of misunderstanding.

Respecting Jurisdictional Boundaries

One state's rule about witness numbers or signatures may not match another's. The steps above fit most places, but always double-check your local laws. You can do this by visiting your government's probate or courts website. Public law libraries or self-help centers have up-to-date guides you can use, and if you hit a snarl, a short meeting with a lawyer gives peace of mind your will is airtight.

Outlining Intentions: Keeping Everything Organized

Mapping out your wishes helps get your will from idea to finished document. Start with a worksheet or a list. Organize what you own and who should get each thing. Don't leave out digital accounts, computers, family photos, or collectibles. If you have pets or want to give something to charity, spell that out. If your child is young, name a guardian—and a backup. Keeping these sections organized prevents headaches for your loved ones.

For instance:

- House and land: Address, who gets it
- Vehicles: Make/model, recipient
- Personal belongings: Jewelry, art, digital assets
- Guardianship for children: Full names of guardians and alternates

Here's how clear plans matter. One family received a will that lumped "all precious things to my kids," but after the testator died, no one could agree what "precious" meant. The fight cost time and money. A neighbor of theirs listed his rare coin collection by year and left it to his niece. No disputes, no delays.

Outlining wishes also sets up the next vital step: choosing an executor. The executor will make sure every instruction you set out in your will happens as intended. Picking the right person for the job is the linchpin for these efforts, which deserves careful thought and planning.

Choosing an Executor: Selecting the Right Person for the Job

After writing out your wishes in a will, one key step remains between intention and reality: choosing the right person to carry them out. A will only works if someone trustworthy is responsible for the details once you're gone. This person is called the **executor**. They serve as the hands and voice of your wishes when you can no longer speak for yourself. The role goes far beyond a title—it determines how smoothly everything unfolds for the people you care about.

An executor's responsibilities extend well beyond sorting through keepsakes. Their first task is to gather information about everything you owned: bank accounts, property, investments, valuables, and debts. Identifying and valuing these assets often involves contacting banks, locating paperwork, and arranging professional appraisals. The executor is also responsible for paying what's owed, including outstanding bills and final taxes. They ensure loans, mortgages, and other debts are resolved, sometimes negotiating with creditors or closing accounts.

Only after these steps can the executor begin distributing what remains to the people named in your will. This might involve writing checks, transferring deeds, or closing accounts. Along the way, the executor works closely with banks, insurance companies, and occasionally the courts, which require official documentation and proof of action. Every step must follow your instructions precisely. The executor carries a legal duty to act fairly, transparently, and without any hint of personal benefit or conflict of interest.

Everyday dilemmas help show how this works. For example, if you owned a family house but still owed money on it, the executor might need to sell the house to pay off what you owed before passing anything on to your children. Sometimes a bank account is forgotten about and found only after searching through old records. These moments demand that the executor stay organized and patient.

A solid executor needs more than family ties. An individual who excels in managing paperwork, pays meticulous attention to detail, and maintains composure in stressful or emotional situations is the ideal choice. Honesty is a must, because people will be watching for fair action. Communication skills help too—relatives may have questions or concerns, and a clear, steady answer keeps mistrust from growing. Another overlooked factor is availability. Someone who lives nearby, who is not overwhelmed with other duties, and who can travel or make calls as needed is better suited than a loved one living across the country or overseas.

People often feel pressure to pick a spouse, eldest child, or close friend simply because of tradition or a personal bond. This sometimes leads to regret if the person is not skilled or available. Choose someone comfortable with financial matters and not afraid to ask for advice. Imagine choosing an executor who dreads paperwork and lets deadlines slip; this can cause missed tax filings, delays that frustrate your heirs, and even penalties. Family conflict is another real risk. For instance, making one child executor over others may trigger resentment, especially if your wishes are complicated or if the family is already divided.

Common pitfalls include picking someone who is absent-minded, overwhelmed, or too emotionally close to make objective choices. There are even cases where the wrong pick leads to endless arguments, the estate sits in limbo, and legal costs drain away much of what you hoped to leave behind.

Cautious decision-making helps prevent these issues. Before naming anyone as executor, have an honest conversation with them. Ask whether they are both willing and able to take on the work, given their own responsibilities and circumstances. In some estates, appointing two co-executors can help share the workload or balance different personalities, but this only works if both people cooperate and communicate effectively. In other cases, it can backfire when co-executors disagree, delaying the entire process. To prepare for the unexpected, name an alternate executor in your will in case your first choice cannot serve.

When it comes time to put this on paper, be precise. State the executor's full legal name and relationship to you. Write clearly: *"I appoint [Name] as the Executor of my will."* If you want two people to serve together, specify: *"I appoint [Name] and [Name] to act as Co-Executors."* Also include a backup plan: *"If [first choice] cannot serve, I appoint [alternate's name] as Executor."* Each instruction should be as clear as the directions used to describe your gifts and other provisions in your will.

By choosing carefully and communicating openly, you make the executor's difficult job manageable—and the aftermath of your passing far smoother for those you love. Preparation like this acts as a shield, protecting your family from confusion, conflict, and unnecessary costs when no will—or no reliable executor—is in place.

Bringing It All Together

Now that you understand the essential role a will plays in protecting your assets and ensuring your wishes are honored, it's time to take action by creating or updating your own. With clear, legally valid instructions and the right executor in place, you can reduce confusion, avoid costly legal battles, and provide peace of mind for yourself and your loved ones. Whether you own a home, care for children, or simply want to leave a thoughtful legacy, having a well-crafted will is a powerful step toward securing the future you envision. This clarity and preparation safeguard your property and lighten the burden on those you care about most when the time comes.

CHAPTER 4
LIVING TRUSTS – THE SECRET WEAPON TO AVOID PROBATE

"You won't have access to your money for months after a loved one dies." That chilling warning came from a friend who had just watched her family struggle through a drawn-out legal battle. She never imagined that settling an estate could be so slow, public, and costly—yet here she was, caught in the middle of court fees, waiting for approval, and worrying about how bills would get paid. Too many families face this reality every year because they didn't know there was another way. What if you could keep control while you're alive, protect your privacy, and, most importantly, spare those you care about from months of uncertainty? The solution lies in a tool many overlook or misunderstand—a living trust. It's not just legal paperwork; it's a carefully designed plan that can smooth the path when life takes unexpected turns. This chapter uncovers how living trusts work, their different forms, and why setting them up properly matters more than you might think.

The Essentials of Living Trusts and Major Types

A living trust is a legal document that lets a person, called the grantor, place their assets—like a house, bank accounts, or investments—under the care of another person, known as the trustee. The trustee manages these assets for the benefit of people that the grantor chooses, who are called beneficiaries. People use living trusts to manage what happens to their property after they pass away, but the benefits often go beyond this simple idea. Imagine a parent with young children who wants to make sure the family home is protected. They can set up a living trust so the house goes straight to their children if something happens to them. In another case, someone caring for an aging parent can put their savings and property in a trust to make sure bills get paid and financial needs are met.

Living trusts give people control while they are alive and offer peace of mind for what happens next. The main reason many families choose a living trust instead of just a will is to avoid probate. Probate is a court-managed process that happens after someone dies. It can be slow, public, and expensive. Probate often takes many months, and sometimes over a year, before loved ones receive what was meant for them. Big court fees and lawyer charges pile up. During this process, family members might wait months to access bank accounts that could help pay bills or manage everyday expenses.

People turn to living trusts because they keep matters private and move more smoothly. When assets are placed in a living trust, the trust—not the individual—owns those assets. After the grantor passes away, the trustee follows the instructions in the trust to transfer assets to beneficiaries. No court is needed to oversee this step, which means families can often take control more quickly. There's no long wait for the judge's approval, and no one outside the family needs to know what is happening. In many cases, this means a spouse or children can cover mortgage payments, medical bills, or other urgent needs without months of legal delays. Suppose a retired couple puts their home and savings into a living trust. If something happens, their children receive what they need to pay for a funeral, cover utility bills, and keep the house running right away.

Living trusts also offer more privacy. A will becomes a public record during probate, so anyone can see its contents. A living trust stays private, only shared with those who need to know. This gives families protection from nosy neighbors, prying relatives, or scammers scanning public court records. It's a quiet, respectful way to manage a family's legacy without putting every detail in front of the world.

Two main types of living trusts exist: revocable and irrevocable. Revocable trust is a flexible choice. The grantor keeps full control over the assets and the trust itself. They can change the trust's instructions, add or take out assets, or even cancel the whole thing at any time as long as they're alive and able. For example, imagine a working couple in their fifties who want to plan for their children's future, but they're not ready to make decisions that cannot be changed. By creating a revocable trust, they can add the family home and savings for now, knowing they can update or change things later if their family grows, they receive an inheritance, or their wishes change.

An irrevocable trust, on the other hand, is more strict. Once it's set up, the grantor cannot easily change or dissolve it. That may sound limiting, but the benefits matter for some families. The assets may be safe from lawsuits or creditors because the grantor no longer legally owns them. If a small business owner worries about legal claims against them, putting assets into an irrevocable trust can shield those assets from being taken in a lawsuit. Or, if a parent has health issues and wants to qualify for certain government benefits, transferring property to an irrevocable trust might help meet eligibility requirements.

Choosing between these trust types depends on how much control someone wants to keep, the risks they face, and their plans for the future. Skipping a trust entirely can lead to painful outcomes—long court battles, higher fees, and the risk that assets go to unintended people. Understanding the features of both revocable and irrevocable living trusts opens the door to smart estate planning that matches each family's values, goals, and needs. The path to choosing the right trust involves learning how each works and thinking carefully about what matters most for one's legacy and loved ones.

Comparing Revocable vs Irrevocable Trusts and Funding Your Trust

Choosing the right living trust means learning the practical trade-offs that can affect how you handle your own assets and protect your family. Living trusts come in two main types—revocable and irrevocable—and knowing the difference between them sets the stage for all the decisions that follow.

Revocable vs. Irrevocable: What Changes in Real Life

A revocable trust lets you stay in control. You can change the rules any time, add or remove property, or even end the trust if your needs shift. For example, a parent who wants to keep full say over a family home or investments while avoiding probate later will favor a revocable trust. This flexibility gives peace of mind but comes with certain limitations. Assets in a revocable trust remain yours for legal and tax purposes. If you owe debts, creditors can access the trust, and the assets are taxed as part of your estate.

Choosing an irrevocable trust means giving up more control—in exchange, you lock in powerful protections. Once set up, an irrevocable trust cannot be changed or dissolved unless the law or beneficiaries allow it. For someone facing looming legal claims or those looking to protect assets against nursing home costs, this can make sense. The moment you move property into an irrevocable trust, it no longer is yours directly. These assets are much more difficult for creditors to access, and depending on your state and timing, they might be exempt from estate taxes. Yet this loss of control is real: you can't take the assets back or change the terms easily. Choosing your type of trust is about lining up these pros and cons with your main goals.

Steps to Setting Up a Living Trust

The process of creating a living trust is clear and manageable when broken into actionable steps.

1. **Take stock of your assets**

Start by listing everything you wish to protect or pass on.

Homeowners often include their primary residence, a vacation cabin, or rental houses.

Families might write down checking and savings accounts, retirement plans, or investments such as stocks and bonds.

Collectors should not forget items with value, such as art, jewelry, or even vehicles.

2. **Choose between a revocable and irrevocable trust**

Your choice here shapes control, protection, and future options.

- If you want the ability to switch things up as life changes, a revocable trust keeps all doors open.
- If your main focus is shielding assets from lawsuits or government claims, then an irrevocable trust can provide that barrier, but you must be ready to hand over the reins for good.

3. **Pick your trustee**

The trustee manages the assets for the benefit of your chosen heirs.

Common picks include yourself (for revocable trusts), your spouse, or a dependable adult child. If your situation is more complex, you may want a professional or a trusted legal advisor. Always consider honesty, reliability, and an understanding of your wishes.

4. **Meet with an estate planning professional**

DIY trust forms exist, but laws differ between states. Legal missteps could cancel out your efforts. An expert helps craft documents that match your unique needs and are valid under local rules.

5. **Draft the trust document**

The trust spells out what assets will be managed, who benefits, and what happens under different circumstances. It should account for children, blended families, or key milestones, like when an heir turns eighteen.

6. **Sign and notarize the trust**

Formal signing by you and sometimes the trustee is required. Most states require a notary's stamp.

7. **Fund the trust: move assets into it**

This step makes the trust real. Each asset may need a different method:

- Real estate: Change the deed so the trust owns your home (ask at your county office for the proper forms).
- Bank accounts and investments: Change the account holder's name to the trust. Your bank will supply forms, or you can work with your advisor.
- Other valuables: Title cars, boats, or business shares in the trust's name if possible.

Why Funding Your Trust Matters

Failing to move property with the right paperwork can defeat your entire plan. A house left out of the trust must pass through probate, which adds cost and delay. Bank accounts not retitled stay outside the trust.

Keep a checklist. After funding, review your asset list once a year or after big life changes. Contact banks, investment offices, and government offices for proof that changes went through.

Looking Ahead

Setting up a living trust and putting assets into it is only part of the picture. Following the practical steps reduces risk, but pay attention to myths and common slip-ups that threaten your family's future. A little care now paves the way for smoother results and fewer surprises.

Common Misconceptions and Mistakes About Living Trusts

Every year, families hear promises that a living trust will guarantee a smooth transition after death, save money, and eliminate probate headaches. Advertisements call trusts "the magic bullet," and friends share stories of hassle-free inheritances. This confidence in living trusts stems from real advantages that both revocable and irrevocable trusts can offer. Trusts can bypass certain court procedures, provide control, and help organize your wishes. Yet many people fall for myths and make simple mistakes that lead to confusion, wasted time, and financial loss—right when their families need clarity the most.

The belief that creating a living trust completely eliminates probate is widespread. The appeal is obvious: probate sounds slow, expensive, and public. People long for a simple fix. However, a trust only avoids probate for assets that have actually been transferred into it. If your name still appears on a house deed or investment account, those assets remain outside the trust and must go through probate. A common scenario unfolds after someone's death: the family opens the trust expecting immediate access to property, only to discover the home or car was never retitled. The court intervenes, months pass, and legal fees drain the estate—exactly the outcome the trust was meant to avoid.

To prevent this, maintain an updated list of all assets and verify who holds official title. Double-check real estate deeds, vehicle registrations, stocks, bank accounts, and other major property. Many banks require special forms to transfer ownership. Keep written proof each time you add something to the trust. If your living trust doesn't legally "own" an asset, probate may still apply regardless of what the trust document states. Setting a yearly reminder to review property titles and account names provides an added layer of protection.

Another stubborn myth says that living trusts erase every tax. The idea comes from confusion about how trusts operate and a wish to escape estate or income taxes. Some families anticipate that a trust will reduce all taxes, including those on retirement funds and capital gains. The truth is, a revocable living trust does not remove assets from your taxable estate while you are alive because you still control everything inside. Irrevocable trusts function differently, but living trusts most often do not change your tax status.

The trap here results in unexpected bills. Take a family who puts their vacation home into a revocable trust, then sells it years later. Tax law still applies; capital gains tax comes due just as if they owned it directly. Consider an adult child who inherits a trust and believes there will be no taxes on those funds but then faces IRS penalties for misreporting. To steer clear, ask your attorney or financial advisor which taxes each trust affects. Never assume a trust automatically removes assets from all taxes. If saving on estate or income tax is the goal, you may need other solutions paired with your trust. Make a list of your goals up front, then have an expert walk through them line by line.

A subtle but dangerous mistake happens when people create trust but never fund it. This results from misunderstandings about how trust works in practice. Completing the paperwork makes the job feel like it's done. The trust folder sits on the shelf, but nothing ever moves into its name. Years later, loved ones discover a beautifully written trust that holds nothing, and all the property ends up in probate. The solution is concrete: after signing the trust, gather all ownership documents and follow through with each transfer. Some accounts take minutes at a branch; others, like real estate, need an updated deed filed with the county. Use a checklist, then verify every transfer with bank statements or title documents before storing your trust paperwork.

Neglecting ongoing trustee duties and updates rounds out the list of costly errors. Life is full of changes: marriage, divorce, new children, a new home, or a falling out with a relative. Many believe once they write their wishes into the trust, those choices will always reflect their true intentions. Over time, an outdated trust may leave assets to people no longer in the family, skip a new grandchild, or fail to meet current laws. Old beneficiaries can end up with property that you intended for others. To prevent this, plan to review your trust every two to three years or after big life events. Update your asset schedule and any new accounts. Write down dates of revisions, and make sure everyone who needs the new version gets it.

People often believe that living trusts will fix everything once they sign the documents. In practice, much depends on careful titling, regular updates, and honest checks on facts and goals. A little extra attention now can spare your loved ones confusion and cost later.

Bringing It All Together

Now that you understand the key features, types, and steps involved in setting up a living trust, you are better equipped to take control of your estate plan and protect your family's future. By carefully choosing between revocable and irrevocable trusts, properly funding your trust, and avoiding common mistakes, you can ensure your assets transfer smoothly, privately, and with fewer costs. This knowledge empowers you to make informed decisions that align with your goals and values, giving you confidence that your loved ones will be cared for without unnecessary legal hurdles or delays. Taking action now sets the foundation for a secure legacy and peace of mind for years to come.

CHAPTER 5

APPOINTING KEY PEOPLE – EXECUTORS, GUARDIANS, AND POWER OF ATTORNEY

More than half of all estate plans run into complications because the right people were not chosen or thoroughly prepared to step into key roles when needed. Executors, guardians, and agents with power of attorney hold responsibilities that can shape how smoothly a family weathers difficult times. Selecting individuals for these roles is not just about trust; it requires careful thought about their ability to manage complex tasks, communicate and handle sensitive situations. Without clear conversations and well-defined expectations, even the most thoughtfully prepared plans can lead to confusion, delays, and conflict. This chapter offers guidance to help you make informed choices and ensure those entrusted with your affairs are ready to act with confidence and care.

Selecting the Right Executor and Communicating Expectations

Almost every estate plan depends on selecting someone willing and capable of serving as executor. This person steps in after your death to ensure that the wishes in your will are carried out. The executor gathers assets, pays debts and taxes, manages accounts, files paperwork with the court, ensures bills are settled, and distributes what remains to the people or organizations you've named. For many families, the executor also serves as a bridge between the legal process and those awaiting their inheritance. It's more than just completing paperwork; it's about guiding others through a difficult time with respect and fairness. When choosing an executor, most people think of a trusted family member or friend, though some opt for a lawyer or professional fiduciary for additional support.

Here are the main tasks every executor must handle:

- Collecting financial documents and locating assets like homes, vehicles, investments, and valuables
- Notifying banks, utility companies, government offices, and other involved parties
- Paying outstanding bills, credit cards, mortgages, and taxes
- Keeping clear records of all income and expenses tied to the estate
- Working with the probate court to meet all legal filing deadlines
- Communicating with beneficiaries to let them know where things stand and what comes next
- Distributing assets according to the will only after debts and taxes are settled

Naming just one person as executor can leave an estate plan vulnerable if that person is suddenly unable or unwilling to serve. Life circumstances can change. A chosen executor might move far away, fall ill, decide the responsibility is too much, or even pass away first. Sometimes family relationships take an unexpected turn, and someone once named might not be the right fit later. That is why almost every solid estate plan names a backup—or alternate—executor. The backup steps in if the first person cannot or will not act. Imagine an estate where the only named executor declines the role or becomes unreachable. The family could be left with delays, disputes, or even a judge deciding who takes over. Listing a backup helps avoid extra paperwork and confusion at one of the worst possible times.

Some people ask a close sibling to be their main executor and a trusted longtime friend as backup. Others prefer a mix, such as naming a family member first and a professional second. The most important thing is that everyone named is comfortable with the job and has the right qualities.

When searching for the right executor, focus on trustworthiness and proven reliability. This person must deal with sensitive information and follow instructions exactly. A solid executor notices details, meets deadlines, and stays organized even when under pressure. The best choice is to be open and calm in communicating with others, especially when people are grieving. Fairness helps prevent hurt feelings or arguments among family. Someone who can manage paperwork and take care of practical tasks, from closing accounts to talking to lawyers, will find the job easier. If a brother and sister don't see eye-to-eye or have quarreled for years, neither makes a good executor if the will's beneficiaries include both. Strong emotions or family drama can stall the entire process.

There are a few legal rules. In most states, an executor must be at least 18 years old and not currently in legal trouble. A "felon" is often barred from serving. Some states require the executor to live in the same state as the person whose estate they are handling, or, if they don't, to appoint a state resident as a representative. Laws can change, so readers should always double-check with a local attorney or look up their state's requirements if they suspect their situation might not be typical.

Raising the question with a possible executor often makes people nervous, but being open from the start helps everyone. Respect matters. Pick a relaxed setting and explain what the role involves in plain terms—handling money, making decisions, and dealing with paperwork. Emphasize why you trust them and give them a chance to voice hesitations or ask questions. Bringing copies of your will and a list of important document locations demonstrates trust. Let them know how they might get help from attorneys or accountants, and make sure they understand they don't have to accept the job right away.

Clarity prevents problems. If an executor knows what to expect and agrees to serve, things move forward more smoothly. But when someone is asked only after the death, they may feel confused or pressured. Some families have faced legal delays because an executor refused the job or struggled to find key paperwork. Others have watched old resentments flare up and slow everything down when a loved one never explained their choice. Simple conversations now save complications later.

Choosing responsible people for critical roles starts with the executor, but it doesn't end there. For families with minor children, deciding who will step in as guardian is just as important—asking different questions, but with the same goal: keeping loved ones safe and supported when they need it most.

Appointing Guardians for Minor Children and Having Essential Conversations

Taking steps to choose the right guardian for minor children comes from the same sense of responsibility that guides the choice of an executor. While executors safeguard your assets and wishes, guardians protect your children's growth, health, and security. Where an executor manages paperwork and financial tasks, a guardian's responsibility extends every day—providing care, emotional support, and stable guidance. Children need not just shelter and education but someone devoted to keeping family routines, beliefs, and connections alive.

A guardian steps in if both parents become unable to provide care. This includes everything from getting children to school and doctor appointments to celebrating birthdays in ways that feel familiar. Over the long term, the guardian might steer big decisions: what community they live in, how faith or family traditions are honored, and how relationships with relatives and friends continue. Occasionally a guardianship is short if a parent recovers from illness or injury, but often it covers the rest of the child's youth. The person you choose will have a daily role in shaping everything from your child's confidence to their sense of belonging.

Evaluating Potential Guardians

A strong choice for a guardian is built on more than trust. One practical way to start: make a list of everyone you consider and weigh each candidate against a set of factors, such as

- **Willingness and comfort with the role:** Begin by thinking, "Would this person want to do this?" Some people might feel honored; others may be uneasy or too burdened. Ask yourself, "Can I picture them thriving in this responsibility, or might they struggle?"
- **Beliefs and values:** Does the candidate have views on parenting, discipline, religion, and education that match yours? For example, if you value open communication or regular gatherings with extended family, will the guardian continue those traditions? Imagine a guardian who is patient and nurturing for a sensitive child; that kind of match smooths the transition if the day comes.
- **Parenting style:** Consider how the guardian manages their own children or interacts with others. If a possible guardian is very strict but you use gentle guidance, there may be friction. Observing how this person responds to everyday stresses—bedtime battles, school issues—offers clues about future success.
- **Family dynamics and existing relationships:** Sometimes the "obvious" person may not suit the child's needs. Suppose a close relative tends to tension with your child, while a good friend steps in as a positive influence. Ask, "Is the bond supportive, or would it add new stress?"

- **Financial stability and resources:** While guardians needn't be wealthy, they should be able to provide for basic needs without strain. Your estate can support guardians financially, but a baseline of stability opens more options for the child's experiences and education.
- **Personal health and geographic location:** A thriving guardian invests energy, time, and care. Consider the person's health, age, and living situation. If you want your child to stay in a certain city or near school friends, location matters.
- **Openness to ongoing connection:** The right guardian is not only willing but also able to keep your child linked to extended family, community, and cultural roots.

Approaching the Conversation

When you identify likely choices, prepare for a conversation grounded in respect and care. Start simply. Share why you are considering them and what values guide your choice. Outline basic expectations, such as where the child might live, day-to-day routine details, and hopes for education or religious upbringing. Encourage honest questions and concerns. Simple language works best:

- "We'd like you to consider taking this role if something happens to us, and we want to talk through what it might look like."
- "Your views about raising kids are close to ours, and we see you as someone who could help them feel safe and loved."

Give the person time to reflect before deciding. Invite their candid thoughts about readiness or reservations. If they feel hesitant, honor that feeling and affirm your trust regardless of the outcome. If there are differing opinions in the family or a strained connection between child and guardian, name it openly and discuss goals: "We value peace and want to avoid tension, but we also believe ___ offers the stability our child would need." Listen for feedback, and where needed, consult a neutral adviser for perspective.

Keeping Plans Clear and Current

Once a guardian agrees, keep the conversation active. Review plans every couple of years or after significant changes—like moving, health issues, or shifts in family structure. Use a letter of wishes, written in plain language, to highlight routines, traditions, bedtime stories, annual trips, or guiding values you hope will stay constant. Deliver this letter with warmth and openness, promising an ongoing dialogue so that no one faces surprises. A thoughtful choice, careful discussion, and shared understanding lay the best foundation for the rest of your planning.

Understanding Powers of Attorney and Discussing Roles with Chosen Agents

Some choices in estate planning need more than just careful thought—they also demand taking action before a crisis. A power of attorney, or POA, stands as one of those legal tools that lets someone else act in your place if you cannot manage things yourself. These documents allow another person—the agent—to step in and handle business or health matters when you are unable to do so. Having both a medical power of attorney and a financial power of attorney in place gives you control over who handles your care, money, and daily affairs at the moments that matter most.

Medical and financial powers of attorney work for separate but vital parts of life. The medical power of attorney allows the agent to make healthcare decisions if illness or injury leaves you unable to speak for yourself. For example, your agent may have to say yes or no to a proposed surgery, discuss treatment plans with doctors, or guide end-of-life care according to your wishes. Nearby hospitals or physicians often require a clear authorization to allow someone else to decide for you. Without a valid medical POA, uncertainty and delay can get in the way of fast treatment.

A financial power of attorney, on the other hand, deals with money and property. Your agent may need to pay bills, manage bank accounts, sign checks, handle insurance matters, or even sell a house while you recover from illness or injury. Real-world situations call for the agent to act while you're in the hospital, in rehab, or facing any situation where you cannot sign a legal document yourself. Having the financial POA in place helps ensure the mortgage gets paid, utilities stay on, and assets remain safe.

Distinctions Between Medical and Financial Powers

Medical and financial POAs may sound similar, but they come with different boundaries and responsibilities. A medical POA does not give the agent access to your bank accounts, just as a financial POA does not let the agent decide about surgeries or medications. Some people choose the same person for both roles, but it's important to match the right person to each set of duties. Communication preferences, personal trust, and availability also factor into these choices.

When Both Are Needed

Imagine an older adult in the hospital after a car accident. A medical POA agent works with doctors to approve surgery and monitor medications, while a financial POA agent handles rent, insurance, and other pressing bills. If both agents do their jobs well, recovery can happen without outside stress or confusion. Skipping one piece often means someone's needs—health or financial—could be overlooked.

Key Qualities for POA Agents

Medical POA agents do best when they can stay calm in emergencies. They need to listen to your wishes, respect your beliefs, and handle tough conversations with healthcare providers. Strong communication helps—so does the ability to speak up under pressure. Being nearby can also make things smoother, as medical decisions often require quick action.

Good financial POA agents need solid money sense. They should be organized, trustworthy, and careful with paperwork. Someone who can stay on top of due dates, keep records, and keep their money separate from yours brings peace of mind. For more complicated estates, someone with an understanding of accounts or investments can be a plus. Some look for a backup—or contingent—agent, naming a second person in case the first cannot serve. This extra step keeps your affairs on track no matter what.

Starting Hard but Honest Conversations

Bringing up these roles can feel awkward, but clear talk saves families from second-guessing later. Try these steps to start the conversation:

- Choose a private, low-stress time to talk.
- Explain why you trust this person for the role: "You've always managed your money carefully, and I want someone level-headed looking out for me."
- Lay out the duty: "This doesn't mean I'm expecting a crisis soon, but I want to be ready."
- Ask if they're comfortable and willing, without pressure.

Use open-ended prompts to guide dialogue:

- "How do you feel about making healthcare choices if I can't speak for myself?"
- "Are you open to stepping in if my finances need daily attention due to illness?"
- "What concerns or questions come to mind about either responsibility?"
- "Would you rather be a backup in case my first choice is unavailable?"

Formalizing Arrangements and Avoiding Conflict

After an honest agreement, get everything in writing. Share the legal documents with your chosen agents and any professionals (like doctors or banks) who may need them. Keep signed copies in an accessible, safe place. Let other family members know your decisions in advance, to head off misunderstandings.

Check back every so often: health, relationships, and trust can all change. Keeping documents and instructions up-to-date, along with ongoing talks, builds the foundation for smooth support if life takes a sudden turn. Early, open planning steers everyone through hard moments with less confusion and more confidence.

Bringing It All Together

Now that you understand how vital it is to choose the right people for key roles in your estate plan—and to communicate their responsibilities clearly—you can take confident steps to protect your family's future. By carefully selecting trustworthy executors, guardians, and agents for powers of attorney who are prepared and willing to serve, you reduce the risk of confusion, delays, or disputes when it matters most. Open conversations and regular updates ensure everyone involved knows what to expect and can act smoothly when called upon. With these tools and thoughtful choices in place, you can move forward knowing your wishes will be honored, your loved ones supported, and your estate handled with care and respect.

CHAPTER 6

MEDICAL DIRECTIVES AND END-OF-LIFE PLANNING

When faced with serious illness or unexpected medical emergencies, having clear instructions about your healthcare wishes becomes essential. Many people avoid thinking about these situations until they arise, but without preparation, decisions can become confusing and stressful for both patients and their families. Knowing how to communicate your preferences in advance protects your rights and provides peace of mind, ensuring that your values guide the care you receive even when you cannot speak for yourself.

This chapter will explore how to formalize your healthcare decisions through important legal documents such as living wills, advance directives, and Do Not Resuscitate (DNR) orders. It will explain how these tools work together to make your wishes known and respected. You will also learn about the role of organ donation preferences in end-of-life planning and practical steps to create, finalize, and store these documents properly. By understanding these elements, you can take control of your medical future and help secure the well-being of your loved ones.

Living Wills, Advance Directives, and DNR Orders: Formalizing Your Healthcare Decisions

Serious medical decisions can arrive with little warning. When a person cannot speak for themselves, having clear instructions in place helps avoid confusion and protects the right to choose the type of care received. Medical directives are written legal documents that spell out these wishes. There are several kinds that work together: living wills, advance directives, and Do Not Resuscitate (DNR) orders. Each serves a different role, but all share the goal of making sure a person's preferences are honored in moments when it matters most.

A **living will** is a document that explains what kinds of medical treatment a person does or does not want if they become unable to communicate, often due to serious illness or injury. For example, a living will may state whether a person wants life-prolonging treatments such as a feeding tube, mechanical ventilation, or dialysis if they are in a coma or a persistent vegetative state. Some include preferences for pain management, even if it could shorten life, or instructions to avoid certain procedures entirely. The document only takes effect once doctors determine that the person cannot make decisions on their own.

Many families have endured long, stressful hospital stays when loved ones had no written guidance. Disagreements can easily arise among siblings or spouses about what a parent would have wanted, with no clear answer. But when a properly signed living will is in place, the family and care team know exactly how to proceed.

Advance directives are broader legal instructions that can include a living will but often go further. In most states, an advance directive lets you appoint a trusted person—a health care proxy, agent, or medical power of attorney—who can legally make health decisions on your behalf if you cannot. These instructions can outline what treatments are acceptable, who may be involved in decisions, and which hospitals or doctors you prefer.

Advance directives are especially valuable in cases of sudden incapacity, such as a stroke or major accident, as well as during long-term illness. For example, imagine a teacher who names his son as his agent in an advance directive. When he unexpectedly collapses and is hospitalized, doctors know to turn to his son for decisions rather than leaving the family uncertain or waiting for a court to intervene. Missing or unclear directives can lead to unwanted tests, prolonged treatments the person never would have chosen, or lasting regret among family members.

A Do Not Resuscitate order (DNR) addresses a single decision: whether to use cardiopulmonary resuscitation (CPR) if a person's heart or breathing stops. This document is often completed in hospitals, nursing homes, or with the help of a doctor for people with advanced illness. For many, a DNR brings comfort by signaling a desire for a natural death, wishing to avoid medical interventions that can be painful or unlikely to work. Others may decide against a DNR, wanting every attempt at revival regardless of their condition. A DNR must be clear and present in the patient's file or posted in the care facility; otherwise, EMS or doctors usually provide full resuscitation by law.

Some people believe that having a **living will** means they don't need an **advance directive**, or that a **Do Not Resuscitate (DNR)** order makes the other documents unnecessary. These are common misunderstandings. A living will records treatment preferences but may not cover every situation or unexpected event. An advance directive adds a trusted decision-maker and additional instructions, offering broader protection. A DNR applies only to CPR decisions and doesn't address other care, such as comfort measures or feeding tubes. Each document complements the others, creating a detailed and flexible plan that reflects a person's values and needs.

Common questions often arise. *"Can I change these documents later?"* Yes. Medical directives can be updated or revoked at any time, as long as you're able to make your own decisions. *"What if my family disagrees with my wishes?"* As long as the documents meet state legal standards, health care providers are required to follow them even if family members object. *"What if my medical situation isn't covered?"* Naming a health care agent through an advance directive ensures that your preferences are represented by someone who knows you well.

Lives are made easier when people take the time to create and update these directives. Families avoid unnecessary heartache, and patients receive care that truly matches their wishes. This is part of a broader process—careful, thoughtful planning for the end of life. Alongside medical choices, it can also include reflecting on your legacy and considering the meaningful act of organ or tissue donation.

Organ Donation Preferences: Making Your Wishes Known

Taking charge of your medical decisions starts with spelling out treatment preferences, but the same sense of control also lets you make choices about organ and tissue donation. When you include organ donation in your planning, you shape what happens to your body in a way that can help others and keep your beliefs front and center. This extends your ability to direct your care and legacy, even in moments when decisions happen quickly and you cannot speak for yourself.

What Organ and Tissue Donation Means

Organ donation means giving permission for doctors to remove organs or tissues from your body after death, usually to save someone else's life or improve their health. Commonly donated organs include the heart, lungs, kidneys, liver, pancreas, and intestines. Tissues such as corneas, skin, bone, heart valves, and tendons also help people. For example, a single donor's organs can help up to eight different people. Tissue donation may allow someone blinded by injury to see again or help a burn victim heal and regain mobility. Donated organs and tissue can give families waiting for transplants hope in accidents that claim lives.

For organ donation to happen, you usually need to pass away in a hospital while on life support, because the organs must be kept healthy until they are recovered. Tissue donation has broader circumstances, since many tissues stay useful for hours even after the heart stops. Both forms offer a final act of care, turning tragedy into new chances for others.

Range of Choices

You can decide to:

- Donate all organs and tissues allowed by law.
- Donate only certain organs or tissues you choose, such as kidneys or corneas.
- Decline all organ or tissue donation.

Some people want to set limits based on their beliefs, family history, or views about illness and death. For instance, a person might feel comfortable donating their corneas but not their heart. Others only want to donate if doctors determine their body can help in a meaningful way. All of these choices are valid and respected when they are clear.

Values, Beliefs, and Traditions

Religious and cultural beliefs play a strong role in donation decisions. Some faiths view organ donation as a final act of charity, such as many Christian and Jewish traditions that encourage helping others, while some Muslim leaders support giving as long as it does not harm the body unnecessarily. Other groups may discourage it, either because of rules about burial or beliefs about the body after death. Sometimes, misunderstandings or stories within a family also guide views. For example, one family may uphold a tradition of giving, while another values keeping the body whole. You do not have to follow any example but your conviction. You can seek advice from your faith leader or a trusted elder if you wish.

How to Register and Document Your Wishes

Registering your decision is easy and gives it the power of law in most states. Most people sign up through their state's Department of Motor Vehicles (DMV), which adds a tag or symbol to your driver's license. You can also join your state's or a national donor registry online or by phone. These steps connect your preferences to the official records that doctors consult during an emergency. Still, listing your wishes in your medical directive or living will keep your decisions tied to your other care instructions. Add clear statements like "I wish to donate my organs and tissues," or list only those you are willing to give.

Many think doctors ignore care if you are an organ donor, but this is false. Doctors who treat you in an emergency work to save your life, no matter your donor status. Only after death does the organ recovery team review your registration. People with cancer, diabetes, or other illnesses can still donate some tissues or organs, depending on their condition. Never decide based on old myths. Always ask your doctor if you have questions about your health and donation.

Talking With Loved Ones

Making a donation can feel personal and emotional. Still, it helps avoid confusion and conflict later if everyone hears your wishes from you directly. Use stories to show why the choice matters. For instance, you might talk about a neighbor who received a heart transplant or how your own family values giving. Invite questions and give time for feelings to surface. Sometimes, writing a short note or recording a message supports your plan. People involved in your care—such as your healthcare proxy, adult children, or close friends—should understand and agree to honor your decision.

Next Steps for Complete Clarity

Organ donation is one part of the bigger picture. Recording this choice points the way to writing down all your end-of-life care wishes and keeping your directives safe and accessible. Just as conversations about donation protect your intent, honest, careful documentation will safeguard every important medical choice when the time comes.

Creating, Finalizing, and Storing Medical Directives: Practical Implementation Steps

Clear and open communication about organ donation is a meaningful act for both you and your family. By deciding and documenting your intentions, you protect loved ones from the stress of having to guess or disagree during a high-pressure moment. All medical directives share this basic purpose—making your choices known, reducing confusion, and ensuring your voice is heard when you might otherwise be silent.

Keeping your medical wishes confined to conversations is not enough. Documents like a living will, an advance directive, a Do Not Resuscitate (DNR) order, and an organ donation statement should exist in forms that doctors and hospitals can legally follow. Each directive covers a unique part of your care:

- **Living Will:** States what types of life-sustaining treatments you want—or don't want—if you become unable to communicate, such as feeding tubes, breathing machines, or CPR.
- **Advance Directive:** Covers a broader scope than a living will, allowing you to select a trusted person (a healthcare proxy or agent) who will make medical decisions for you if you are unable.

- **DNR Order:** Tells health professionals you do not want attempts at resuscitation if your heart or breathing stops. This must be a formal, signed medical document recognized by hospitals and emergency responders.
- **Organ Donation Statement/Card:** Expresses your wish to donate organs or tissue after death. This can appear on your driver's license, a standalone card, or a written statement.

Getting these forms is simple. Start with your state's health department website or ask your doctor's office. Hospitals often provide them for free. Reputable nonprofit organizations online, like the National Hospice and Palliative Care Organization or state bar associations, offer downloadable versions. Always use the version valid in your state—small details can differ.

You usually need to be an adult, and some states require that you are of sound mind when signing. Read each form closely. Be sure to fill in every section thoroughly, choosing clear, plain answers to questions about treatments or your choice of decision-maker. Never leave blanks—gaps may cause confusion or invalidate the document. For the living will, spell out unexpected details. For example, if you wish to refuse a feeding tube but still want comfort care, specify that.

For your directives to stand up in an emergency or legal setting, follow your state's full requirements about signing, witnessing, and notarizing. Most forms must be signed by you and witnessed by one or two adults. These people should not be named as your agent, heirs, or doctor—pick witnesses with no "stake." Some states require a notary stamp. As you sign, double-check that all boxes are filled, names are spelled right, and the right people are present.

Missing a witness or using the wrong form can undo all your planning. Imagine a person signs a living will and thinks it is valid, but both witnesses are family heirs. In a crisis, doctors may set aside the document because state law forbids heirs from witnessing. The result: your medical decisions could go against your wishes. To avoid this, ask a nurse, social worker, friend, or neighbor who is not included in your will to witness. Review every page against state requirements before considering it done.

Where and how you keep these papers matters. Store original documents in a fireproof home safe or a locked file, rather than in a hard-to-access safety deposit box. Give signed copies to your main doctor, designated healthcare agent, and local hospital for their files. Some people upload digital scans to a secure online health portal or emergency document service. It helps if you carry a simple wallet card stating you have advance directives, with clear contact information for your healthcare agent or the location of your documents.

Share your signed directives with everyone who needs to know: doctors, the person you named as your decision-maker, and close family. Do not assume they will always know where to look. Using digital registries—either provided by your state or a major healthcare system—can ensure hospital staff access your forms in a crisis.

Review your directives every few years, or after major changes like marriage, divorce, a new diagnosis, or moving. Check with your healthcare agent that they are still able and willing to honor your wishes. To start a conversation, you might say, "I want to talk about my wishes for medical care if I can't speak for myself. There are forms I filled out, and here's what they mean." Or with doctors: "I have an advance directive and living will. Let's make sure you have them on file."

Simple, well-prepared documents, shared with those who count, save loved ones from stress and uncertainty—and make sure your choices are honored.

Concluding Thoughts

Now that you understand the importance and distinct roles of living wills, advance directives, DNR orders, and organ donation statements, you can take confident steps to formalize your healthcare decisions. By creating, updating, and securely storing these documents, and by sharing them clearly with those who matter most, you protect your wishes from confusion or dispute when you cannot speak for yourself. This proactive planning safeguards your rights and eases the burden on loved ones during difficult times. Moving forward, make it a priority to review your directives regularly and communicate openly, ensuring your medical care and legacy reflect your values and choices with clarity and respect.

CHAPTER 7

MINIMIZING TAXES AND LEGAL COSTS

Many people believe estate planning is simply about deciding who inherits their belongings, but the reality is far more complex—and costly. If you don't carefully consider taxes and legal fees, you risk losing a significant portion of your assets before they reach your loved ones. This chapter challenges the assumption that estate planning is only for the wealthy and reveals how strategic steps can help families of all sizes protect what matters most.

This chapter explores practical ways to minimize the impact of estate taxes and reduce legal expenses through thoughtful planning. It guides you through understanding key tax concepts, using trusts effectively, managing legal costs, and integrating life insurance into your plan. By focusing on these areas, you can safeguard your family's financial future while avoiding unnecessary burdens and fees.

Understanding Estate Taxes and Tax-Saving Tools

Estate planning isn't only about deciding who gets what—it's about making sure more of what you own actually reaches the people you care about. For most adults managing their homes, savings, and retirement accounts, keeping more of their assets in the family often means learning the basics of taxes and costs that come with handling an estate. Knowing how taxes work and the smart moves you can make will help you avoid surprises, fight off extra expenses, and give your family the peace of mind they deserve.

Estate taxes rarely apply to most families, but understanding them gives you a sense of control. An estate tax is a tax on your total assets at death, before they go to heirs. This is different from an inheritance tax, which some states charge when someone actually receives money or property, and different again from the gift tax, which is triggered if you give away too much in a single year or over your lifetime. The federal estate tax only applies to estates valued over $12.92 million as of 2023. That number means most Americans won't pay a federal estate tax at all. For example, if your total assets—such as your house, retirement accounts, cars, investments, and even personal items—add up to under $12.92 million when you die, the federal government will not take a portion through estate tax.

Some states set their estate tax rules, and their thresholds are often much lower than the federal level. For instance, Massachusetts and Oregon impose estate taxes that begin on estates valued between $1 million and $2 million. If you live in or own property within one of these states, it's important to understand both state and federal regulations to see whether your assets could be affected. Even if the federal threshold seems far off, the value of your home or life insurance could push your total assets higher—especially in high-cost areas or after years of appreciation.

Consider two common examples. The first is a couple in their sixties who own a home valued at $450,000, have $300,000 in retirement savings, and have around $50,000 in other investments and cash. Their total estate, at roughly $800,000, falls well below the $12.92 million federal limit, so they won't owe federal estate taxes. Unless they live in a state with a lower threshold, estate taxes are unlikely to affect their plan.

The second example involves a family that owns a business, several investment properties, and homes in two different states worth about $8 million, along with retirement and investment accounts. Their total estate approaches—or exceeds—both federal and state limits. Without proper planning or professional guidance, a significant portion of their wealth could go to taxes instead of their heirs. Families who receive large inheritances, build successful businesses, or hold substantial life insurance policies can sometimes find their estates growing into taxable territory without realizing it.

Small actions now can keep more assets in your family's hands. One of the strongest ways to lower possible estate taxes is creating a trust. A trust is a legal arrangement where you transfer assets to a trustee, who then manages those assets for your chosen beneficiaries (like children). Trusts come in different types. A revocable living trust lets you keep control and change things if needed, but the assets still count toward your estate's value for tax purposes. An irrevocable trust means giving up control—you can't simply take things back—but the assets placed inside do not count toward your taxable estate anymore. A family with a high-value life insurance policy may place it in an irrevocable trust, removing the payout value from their taxable estate and handing it more cleanly to children.

Some parents create a special needs trust for a child, both to provide for lifelong care and to keep those funds separate from taxes or limits that apply to direct assets. Charitable trusts help by donating to a cause, letting you lower the taxable amount and support something you believe in at the same time.

Giving gifts during your life is another way to lower estate taxes. The IRS allows you to give up to $17,000 to someone in 2023 without paying gift tax or reducing your lifetime exemption. That means a couple could give $17,000 each to each of their children, every year, passing down wealth and reducing the value of their estate for tax purposes. If your estate may grow near the limit, giving some away early can make a meaningful difference.

Tax-advantaged accounts help on another front. IRAs, 401(k)s, and 529 college savings plans all allow you to name a beneficiary. When you do this, those assets can pass directly to your chosen person without going through probate, sometimes skipping state estate tax or lowering exposure. For example, naming your spouse as the beneficiary on your IRA lets those funds go straight to them; no court involvement is needed. Taxes on certain account withdrawals still apply, but naming beneficiaries avoids delays and legal fees connected to probate.

Taxes are not the only factor that can eat up your family's legacy. Legal costs and fees can shrink an estate if planning is ignored or done in a hurry. Paying attention to both taxes and fees is step one in building an estate plan that truly protects your family's wellbeing and wealth for the long run.

Managing and Reducing Legal Costs

Families often hear about estate tax planning, but costs can also mount from the legal side if not carefully managed. Protecting assets and ensuring wishes are honored means understanding not only where legal bills lurk but also how to cut them down to size. Care in this area lets more of your assets go to loved ones, easing their burden when the time comes.

Types of Legal Costs in Estate Planning

Legal expenses in estate planning come in several forms. Some are upfront and easy to see, while others hide in the details and unexpected events.

- **Attorney fees** stand out as the most visible cost. These may be:
  - **Hourly**: The lawyer charges for each hour spent on your matter. Complex families or several rounds of revisions make this cost rise fast.

    - **Flat fees**: For set services, like simple wills or power of attorney documents, the lawyer quotes a price before work starts.
    - **Percentages**: Sometimes, for managing estates through probate, lawyers may charge a percentage of the total estate value, which can add up when assets are high.
- **Court filing fees** come into play whenever documents need to be officially filed, such as for probate proceedings or guardianships.
- **Document preparation charges** apply even for standard paperwork. Fees can rise if revisions or additions are needed after the initial documents are created.
- **Specialized services** increase the bill. These might include setting up complex trusts, arranging durable power of attorney, or handling advance healthcare directives.
- **Extra or unexpected expenses** show up when documents need amendments, when family disputes arise and spark litigation, or if appraisals must be done for property or family businesses.

Common Cost Traps

Failing to keep legal documents up-to-date is one reason costs spiral. Changes after a marriage, divorce, birth, or significant financial event can require new paperwork, which almost always brings another round of fees. Disagreements between heirs trigger court battles, often making legal costs skyrocket. Unorganized executor appointments result in errors and delays, which invite hours of legal work and additional costs.

Practical Steps to Reduce Legal Expenses

You don't have to accept high bills as a given. Simple actions before and during the estate planning process can save real money.

- **Prepare thoroughly before meeting a professional**
  - Gather all relevant documents: deeds, lists of assets and debts, insurance policies, account statements, and personal identification.
  - Set estate goals: who gets what, who can act for you, and any special requests.
  - Decide who could serve as executor, trustee, or power of attorney based on their organizational and financial skills.
- **Communicate goals from the start**
  - Explain wishes and priorities in the first meeting to avoid unnecessary follow-up sessions.
  - List questions in advance instead of asking them one at a time over several phone calls or emails.
- **Use technology when possible**
  - Reputable online legal platforms allow for simple wills and advance directives at a fraction of the cost of in-person lawyers.
  - For example, a young couple with plain wishes might use an online service to draft wills, but if they own a business or have a blended family, a paid consultation with an attorney remains worthwhile.
- **Ask about fees up front**
  - Get quotes for flat-fee services whenever possible, limiting uncertainty.
  - Compare lawyers or planning firms by their approach to billing—some may offer package deals, while others bill hourly or take a percentage.

- **Leverage community and group resources**
  - Many legal aid clinics, senior centers, or employee assistance programs offer discounted or even free help with estate planning basics.
  - Unions, alumni networks, or professional organizations sometimes provide access to vetted attorneys at special rates.

Illustration: Organized Family, Lower Bill

Imagine a family that reviews and organizes all their account statements, property records, and insurance in advance. They come to the attorney with a clear list of goals and executor choice. This preparation means their lawyer spends less time sorting through paperwork or clarifying intentions, reducing billable hours and keeping the process efficient.

Strategies to Simplify and Avoid Legal Tangles

- Keep beneficiary designations up-to-date on retirement accounts, life insurance policies, and payable-on-death bank accounts. These assets move directly to heirs and often bypass legal wrangling.
- Use joint ownership with rights of survivorship, where appropriate, so property passes directly to the surviving owner.
- Avoid overcomplicating trusts or setting up unnecessary entities unless there are clear benefits. Complexity can lead to confusion, mistakes, and hours of legal fixes.
- Pick executors and powers of attorney for their skills, not just family ties, to cut down on confusion and avoid costly delays.

Planning in this way not only brings peace of mind, but it also shields families from financial shocks at an already stressful time. Looking ahead, the next step involves fitting in financial products such as life insurance to further guard against risks that pure legal planning can't always cover, making sure heirs receive support with less hassle and uncertainty.

Incorporating Life Insurance into Estate Planning

Expenses often follow a person's death, leaving families with sudden legal bills, taxes, or debts that must be settled quickly. Life insurance provides families the cash they need immediately after death, offering an effective way to limit the stress of selling off assets or homes at a loss. When a person passes, life insurance payouts are typically released directly to named beneficiaries. This step bypasses probate, which can drag on for months and generate legal costs. The direct payment of insurance proceeds helps families settle medical bills, funeral costs, mortgages, and estate taxes quickly. Instead of waiting for a court to sort out the estate, families can address these expenses immediately. Having cash available prevents heirs from needing to sell family property, stocks, or treasured items during a tough time.

Life Insurance Benefits for Heirs and Tax Reduction

The death benefit from a life insurance policy also keeps the long-term financial goals of the family in focus. These funds can serve as a bridge for daily expenses, pay for college, or keep up on the mortgage. It's a flexible source of money when heirs might have no other quick access to funds. For example, a family with young children might use the policy's proceeds to fund tuition or childcare. For a couple, the surviving spouse could use insurance to cover monthly bills or retirement savings. This security lessens the chance that surviving family members will face missed opportunities or sudden hardship.

There's also a tax benefit. In most cases, death benefits from life insurance paid to individuals are not counted as taxable income on the federal level. This means heirs receive the full sum without needing to set aside a chunk for the IRS. But estate taxes may apply if the insured owns the policy and the value of the overall estate, including the insurance, crosses a federal estate tax threshold. Some states have their estate or inheritance taxes, which can also affect the payout.

How a policy is owned and who is named as beneficiary makes a difference. To avoid adding insurance proceeds to a taxable estate, many people set up an irrevocable life insurance trust (ILIT). The trust owns the policy; after death, proceeds go to the trust, then to beneficiaries, staying out of the taxable estate.

Example Scenario

Imagine a single parent, Sarah, who owns a $500,000 policy. If she is the owner and the beneficiary is her adult daughter, the payout will be taxed only if Sarah's overall estate is large enough for estate taxes to kick in. Sarah wants to avoid this. She creates an ILIT, which owns the policy. After Sarah's death, her daughter gets the money from the trust without extra estate taxes.

Types of Life Insurance in Estate Planning

Choosing the right life insurance depends on long-term goals and cost. There are two broad types:

- **Term Life Insurance** covers a set period—like twenty years. If death happens during the term, the payout goes to the beneficiaries. These policies are usually less expensive, but once the term ends, coverage and benefits go away. Term insurance often works best for short-term needs or debts with an end date, such as a mortgage.

- **Permanent Life Insurance** (including whole and universal life) doesn't expire if premiums are paid. These policies build cash value over time and guarantee a death benefit no matter when the insured passes away. Permanent insurance costs more but offers certainty for estate planning goals.

For estate planning, permanent policies are favored because they guarantee a payout. For example, John and Lisa want to ensure they leave something for their three children regardless of when they pass. They choose a whole life policy, even though it's pricier. The security outweighs extra premium dollars. On the other hand, Maria, age 44, with two young kids and a tight budget, obtains a twenty-year term policy just to cover her mortgage and childcare while the kids are dependent. For people looking to create a legacy for years to come, permanent insurance better fits the goal.

Integration with the Larger Estate Plan

Life insurance policies work best when woven into the full estate plan. Many people name a trust as the policy's beneficiary. This allows the terms of the trust to control how and when the money gets handed out. For those wanting to support a cause, designating a charity as a beneficiary delivers donations while reducing estate size and possibly lowering taxes. Policy reviews matter, too. Updates may be needed after a birth, death, marriage, or divorce.

Smart use of life insurance brings peace of mind. It offers protection from unexpected taxes, legal bills, or asset sales, supporting every step taken to keep more wealth in the hands of beneficiaries. Careful planning matches the right policy and ownership methods to the needs of each family, reinforcing asset protection and trimming long-term costs.

Bringing It All Together

Now that you understand how estate taxes, legal fees, and life insurance affect your family's financial future, you can take confident steps to protect your assets and reduce unnecessary costs. By planning carefully—using tools like trusts, updating documents regularly, choosing the right beneficiaries, and exploring life insurance options—you can keep more of your estate in your family's hands and avoid costly surprises. This proactive approach not only saves money but also brings peace of mind, ensuring your loved ones are supported without added stress or delays. Taking action today means building a stronger, clearer legacy for tomorrow.

CHAPTER 8
PROTECTING REAL ESTATE AND PROPERTY

The call came late one evening: a family member had passed away unexpectedly, and the house they left behind was suddenly at the center of confusion and conflict. Titles were unclear, documents were scattered, and what should have been a simple transfer of ownership turned into weeks of legal wrangling. Feeling overwhelmed, those left behind soon realized how little they understood about protecting such a valuable asset—and how costly that lack of preparation could become.

This moment is not uncommon. Too often, families lose time, money, and peace because basic steps weren't taken to secure property in advance. But what if there were clear ways to prevent this chaos—tools to organize ownership and strategies to protect assets from unexpected risks? The process may seem complicated, yet with the right guidance and a few deliberate actions, it becomes manageable—providing peace of mind that your property is safeguarded today and ready for tomorrow's uncertainties.

Primary Methods for Safeguarding Property: Trusts, Joint Ownership, and Transfer-on-Death Deeds

Trusts serve as a cornerstone for shielding real estate, providing a way for property owners to avoid probate, increase privacy, and manage their assets both while living and after passing away. Placing a property in a trust involves creating a legal arrangement where someone (the trustee) holds title to the property for the benefit of another person (the beneficiary). One of the most common and practical options is a living revocable trust. In this setup, the property owner usually acts as both trustee and beneficiary during their lifetime, keeping full control of the asset. If incapacity strikes, a successor trustee steps in, allowing for uninterrupted management. When the owner passes away, the successor trustee distributes the property to the named beneficiaries without sending it through probate court.

Setting up a trust starts with choosing the right kind for the owner's goals, most often a revocable living trust for homes intended to pass smoothly to family. The property title changes from the owner's name to the name of the trust, a step that must be reflected in the deed recording. Trust documents must name the trustee and successor trustee and list the beneficiaries. The process centralizes management and control, particularly useful for those with young children, blended families, or anyone who wants to avoid court involvement. Control also extends to possible protection from some creditors who might otherwise target the property. Typically, creating a trust involves some legal paperwork and fees, but the later reduction in court and attorney costs often outweighs these costs.

An example brings this home: a parent sets up a revocable living trust, names their child as the beneficiary, and retitles the family house to the trust. Should the parent pass away or become incapacitated, the successor trustee takes over. When the parent dies, the house passes straight to the child, skipping probate and minimizing both delays and disputes.

Joint ownership takes a different approach, relying on co-ownership arrangements that transfer property automatically at death. There are several ways to structure joint ownership. Joint tenancy with right of survivorship means that when one owner dies, the surviving owner instantly holds full title. Tenancy by the entirety applies to married couples in some states, providing similar survivorship rights along with added protection from creditors. Tenancy in common, while allowing shared ownership, does not ensure automatic transfer or survivorship; each owner can instead pass their fractional share to beneficiaries in their will.

The primary advantage of joint tenancy and tenancy by the entirety lies in their straightforward nature. Once established by titling the deed correctly, no extra paperwork or legal action is needed after one co-owner dies. Ownership simply continues with the survivor, trimming away court fees and delays. These structures are affordable to set up, because transferring to joint ownership is often just a matter of recording a new deed. Yet practical risks exist. If one co-owner faces lawsuits, divorces, or debts, the property could be at risk from their creditors. Disagreements or changes in family relationships may also create tension or legal fights down the line.

This is seen when two siblings inherit their childhood home as joint tenants. Years later, one passes away. The survivor instantly controls the property, and the house never enters probate, avoiding a tangle of paperwork and family disputes.

Adding to the toolkit, transfer-on-death (TOD) deeds offer a "payable on death" style solution for real estate, now recognized in many states. A TOD deed lets an owner name a beneficiary who will receive the property the moment the owner dies, avoiding probate. Setting one up means filling out a form deed with the correct beneficiary name and recording it at the local land records office. The owner can amend or revoke the deed anytime before death, preserving complete authority during their life.

TOD deeds offer several clear upsides. Property owners keep autonomy, pay few costs, and sidestep the probate system. But pitfalls arise if the owner moves or changes beneficiaries and fails to update the deed. Only a limited number of states allow TOD deeds for real property. For example, a parent records a TOD deed directing their house to a son. Upon the parent's death, the property is transferred directly and immediately to the child without legal battles or any court filings.

Choosing a method starts with personal goals and family needs:

- For those wanting control, privacy, and flexibility for complex families, trusts are the best fit.
- If easy, inexpensive transfer to a spouse or single heir is the goal and all parties get along, joint ownership can work.
- For those who want simple, low-cost solutions and live in a TOD-eligible state, the TOD deed streamlines everything.

Here's a checklist for getting started:

- Decide on the right method for your property and family plan
- Gather key documents and check your state's laws
- Complete all forms, deed transfers, or trust paperwork fully and accurately
- Record documents with your county or city land office
- Review your arrangements every few years or after major life changes

Laying this foundation for the family home means basic risks are handled, making it easier to focus on other properties where extra exposure, debts, or rental rules often matter. Vacation homes and rentals sometimes call for layered or staggered protection using different versions of these strategies.

Protecting Second Homes and Rental Properties: Unique Considerations and Strategies

Protecting a non-primary residence demands a shift in strategy from the approaches used for your main home. While methods such as using a trust, setting up joint ownership, or naming a transfer-on-death beneficiary work well for shielding your primary residence, second homes or investment properties introduce fresh opportunities and new kinds of risks. These homes may sit vacant for stretches, host renters, or operate across state lines, each scenario bringing its set of exposures. Because of this, the protection plan needs to expand and adapt.

Owning a rental property or vacation home can create steady income or serve as a family getaway. Yet, alongside the rewards, these properties introduce new growth, disruption, and uncertainty. Three main risk areas deserve attention: tenant issues, liability from incidents on the property, and challenges driven by the property's region or local law.

Tenant Risks

Tenant issues can cause headaches. Renters sometimes damage property, miss payments, or start legal disputes. To lower these risks, focus first on clear paperwork. A detailed lease agreement spells out the renter's responsibilities, covers security deposit requirements, sets rules about subletting, and describes exactly what counts as property damage. Strong, clear language reduces confusion and gives you a tool to back up claims if something goes wrong.

It helps to include check-in and check-out inspection forms within the lease. These forms record the condition of the rooms, appliances, and fixtures, leaving less room for disagreement. If a renter tries to dispute charges or blame you for damage, the signed documents provide support.

Liability Exposure

Liability risks go beyond everyday wear and tear. Guests, workers, or neighbors could suffer injury while on your property, leading to lawsuits or insurance claims. Holding your real estate through a business entity, like a limited liability company (LLC), can create a shield. With an LLC, legal action against the property stops at the business and typically cannot reach your personal assets.

Setting up an LLC requires registration with your state and regular updates—but the paperwork pays off. For example, an owner who held his duplex in an LLC faced a tenant lawsuit after a slip on icy stairs. Because the LLC owned the duplex, the suit targeted the company and not his family's personal savings or primary home.

Insuring the property properly finishes the shield. Regular homeowners insurance does not always cover rental situations or cover income lost when a vacation property shuts down after storm damage. Landlord insurance fills in those gaps and covers risks from tenants. An umbrella policy stretches liability protection further, often adding millions in extra coverage for a modest cost. If you let friends use your property or rent it out on short-term platforms, ask your insurer about adding riders for those purposes.

A property-specific rider can handle issues unique to your area. After a hurricane, for instance, a vacation homeowner with a storm coverage rider received quick payment for roof repairs, avoiding months of lost income.

Regional Concerns

Local laws can affect your rental or second home. Zoning, noise rules, and restrictions by homeowner associations can lead to fines or forced changes. Short-term rental bans are spreading, while some areas demand extra permits or limit how long tenants can stay.

Stay organized by keeping a copy of all local rules relevant to your address. Reach out to the city or HOA before making changes or renting to check for new requirements.

Titling Ownership and Structure

The way you hold title matters. For a vacation home used only by family, sole or joint ownership may work fine. If you want relatives to inherit it easily, adding the house to a living trust keeps it out of probate court. For rentals, an LLC usually offers more protection. Compare fees, local laws, and how easily you can access equity when picking your structure.

Keep everything current. If you change the use of the property—for instance, switching from family use to regular rental—update the ownership structure, lease forms, and insurance to match.

Action Checklist

- Draft a thorough lease agreement with inspection forms
- Hold rental properties in an LLC for liability protection
- Maintain landlord insurance, property rider, and umbrella policy
- Choose a titling method that matches the specific use and ownership goals
- Gather and update copies of all zoning, permit, and HOA rules
- Review and refresh documents whenever the property's use changes

Careful organization and ongoing updates help each property stay protected under changing circumstances. Keeping all records, coverage, and ownership forms clear will make the next phase—recordkeeping and documentation—much easier and more effective.

Maintaining Security with Proper Documentation: The Importance of Updated and Recorded Paperwork

Keeping property investments safe depends on more than sturdy locks and good insurance. Staying diligent with documentation forms the backbone of property protection, no matter if you own your family home, a vacation house, or a rental property. Properties such as second homes or rentals often come with distinct risks: ownership changes, multiple users, or extended periods where the owner is not present heighten the potential for mistakes or fraud if paperwork falls out of order. A strong habit of reviewing and organizing property records builds a secure foundation that lasts through major life events and changes in ownership.

Property paperwork includes several must-review documents. Deeds and titles prove who owns the property and show its legal description. Mortgage statements reveal any outstanding loans or liens and highlight the financial obligations attached to the property. Insurance policies detail what is covered in the event of damage or disaster. Trust declarations, beneficiary designations, and any amendments document the current legal status and any instructions for future transfer. Also, keep records of property taxes paid, utility bills that establish occupancy, and any documents from county recorders or local governments about your property. Every name, address, date, and legal description should be consistent across all these files. Even a small error, such as a misspelled name or an old address, can lead to confusion or legal hurdles in the future.

Unchecked or outdated paperwork can introduce costly setbacks. For example, if a property deed lists the wrong owner or address, family members may face probate delays or fail to inherit assets as intended. An old mortgage statement that is not replaced after refinancing might misrepresent current debts, slowing down the sale or transfer of a home. An unrecorded transfer to a trust can leave an estate open to legal battle, even if the owner's wishes were clear. Cases like these end up in court, taking months or years to resolve, and often bring high legal costs or lasting friction between heirs. Equally, unmonitored records increase vulnerability to identity theft or fraudulent transfer attempts that can put property ownership at risk.

Making organization a routine stops these problems before they start. Start by creating a master file for each property you own, both in physical form—using a locked file cabinet or safe deposit box—and digitally, with backup copies stored in encrypted cloud accounts or on reliable drives. Group records by type: deeds and titles in one folder, mortgage and lien statements in another, insurance paperwork in a third, and all supporting documents—like tax records and correspondence with officials—in labeled subfolders. Color-coding or using digital tags can help you spot missing paperwork quickly.

Set calendar reminders once or twice a year to review your property files. During each review, confirm that all names appear exactly as they should, dates are current, descriptions match the latest legal survey or appraisal, and supporting bills or receipts have no gaps. If you spot any outdated paperwork, contact the source—whether that's your mortgage company, insurance agent, or county recorder—for an updated version and replace the old documents in your files. Keep a log with each record, noting when it was last reviewed or updated, along with the name and contact information of the official or agent you spoke with.

Original documents, such as signed deeds or trust declarations, deserve special care. Store them somewhere both secure and accessible, such as a fireproof safe at home or a safe deposit box at your bank. Make copies for everyday reference and provide a trusted person, such as your attorney or adult child, instructions on where to find the originals in an emergency.

Some events force updates. If you get married, divorced, or widowed, update deeds, titles, and insurance beneficiaries promptly. After refinancing a mortgage, add the new statement and remove the old one. If you transfer your property into a trust or change a beneficiary, double-check that every record reflects this. When an owner dies, submit required forms to official agencies and request updated documentation showing the rightful new owner or trustee. Waiting can cause complications that delay sales, inheritance, or insurance payouts.

A few warning signs call for immediate review. These include mismatched names or addresses between documents, notifications about liens you did not authorize, errors on statements, or legal papers arriving about your property. Any change in your personal information, like a new last name, also requires careful checking to avoid errors that can spiral into larger issues.

Making these routines a habit is easier with practical systems. Try using cloud storage services with bank-level security for digital copies, investing in a safe deposit box for originals, and reviewing property management or document tracking apps. Develop a checklist of required records so you know at a glance what needs updating. Taking these steps makes property ownership more secure and helps protect your investment—and your loved ones' peace of mind—long into the future.

Final Thoughts

Now that you understand the key strategies and practical steps for protecting your real estate and property assets, you are better equipped to create a secure plan tailored to your family's needs and goals. Whether choosing trusts for control and privacy, joint ownership for simplicity, or transfer-on-death deeds for straightforward transfers, taking action will help you avoid costly legal delays and protect your investment against unexpected challenges. Maintaining accurate, up-to-date documentation and regularly reviewing your arrangements ensures your plan stays strong through life's changes. By applying these tools thoughtfully, you can safeguard your property, reduce stress for your loved ones, and build a lasting legacy with confidence and peace of mind.

CHAPTER 9
DIGITAL ESTATE PLANNING – WHAT HAPPENS TO YOUR ONLINE LIFE?

"Did you ever think about what happens to your email, social media, or online bank accounts if something happens to you? Most of us have dozens of digital accounts that hold more than just passwords—they contain memories, money, and personal information. Yet, many people haven't made plans for who will manage these assets or how they will be protected in the future. As technology becomes a bigger part of our daily lives, understanding how to organize and secure your online presence is no longer optional—it's essential. This chapter guides you through the steps to take control of your digital legacy, so your loved ones won't face confusion or loss when they need access most."

Managing Digital Assets and Setting Up Legacy Access

A **digital asset** is any online record, account, file, or collection connected to your name or finances. These range from online bank accounts and brokerage logins, which hold direct financial value, to cloud services like Google Drive or Dropbox, where family photos or important documents may be stored. Email accounts, utility bill portals, loyalty rewards memberships, streaming subscriptions, and social media profiles are all part of your digital footprint. Some assets, like PayPal or Venmo accounts, contain funds or transaction histories that affect ongoing business or estate matters. Others, such as Facebook pages or digital music libraries, hold personal meaning or purchased content you wouldn't want to lose. It's also easy to overlook domain names, personal websites, and cryptocurrency wallets, yet losing access to them can mean permanent loss of money or irreplaceable memories.

The value of these assets goes far beyond dollars. Personal emails may include family correspondence or legal notifications. Digital photo libraries can represent decades of memories—imagine the heartbreak if no one could retrieve them after a death. Cryptocurrency wallets, protected only by private keys, are often lost forever without proper documentation. It's common for relatives to find themselves unable to unlock a parent's photo backup or locate an account number for a digital brokerage. Even loyalty points, hotel rewards, or frequent flyer miles may be transferable, adding to potential losses when records aren't tracked.

With so many accounts to manage, **password organization** becomes one of the biggest challenges. Many people reuse a few passwords or jot them down on paper, but these methods fail when someone else needs access in an emergency. Frequent resets and varying requirements add confusion. The average person now manages dozens of logins, each demanding strong, unique credentials to reduce the risk of fraud or hacking. Yet while complex passwords keep intruders out, they can also lock out your family.

Password managers help solve this problem. Services like LastPass, 1Password, and Bitwarden create a secure digital vault where every login, password, and note is encrypted and protected by one strong master password that only you know. Inside, you can store credentials for all accounts, generate new passwords, and organize entries by category or use. Many managers allow sharing access with trusted contacts through built-in tools. For estate planning, this vault becomes a kind of master key—if a designated executor knows how to access it, your entire online world remains reachable when needed.

Setting up a password manager usually involves these steps:

1. Choose a reputable password manager and create your account.
2. Choose a long, unique master password you won't forget.
3. Import or manually add credentials for each digital account.
4. Group accounts by category or add notes for context.
5. Enable any "emergency access," "family sharing," or backup features.

It's essential to protect and document your master password or any emergency recovery methods. Keep printed instructions sealed in a safe or lockbox, and consider having a second copy in another secure location. Naming a reliable contact who can assist—preferably someone who understands privacy—helps keep everything accessible in case of urgent need.

Large companies now recognize the importance of digital inheritance. Many major platforms include settings to designate successors or give limited access after an account becomes inactive. For example, Google's Inactive Account Manager lets you choose trusted people to get notified or receive selected data if your account is unused for a period. Facebook allows you to select a Legacy Contact, empowering them to manage your memorialized profile or download shared material. Apple offers a Digital Legacy feature, enabling a nominated person to retrieve your iCloud data after a review period. It's wise to regularly review and update these settings to match changing relationships or asset values. Naming more than one trusted contact lowers the chance that no one can act if the main contact is unavailable.

A solid organizational system supports all of these solutions. Start by listing all digital assets in a spreadsheet, a secure note, or an encrypted file. Categories might be:

- Financial: banks, investments, crypto wallets
- Communication: email, social platforms, chat accounts
- Media: photos, music, book collections
- Utilities and Services: bills, reward programs

Include short notes for each—why it matters, its approximate value, and tips for accessing it. If using hard copies, keep them in a locked drawer or safe deposit box, not in a public spot. Only share these lists, or vault passwords, with individuals who really need access, sticking to the principle of least privilege to limit privacy risk.

Planning these steps protects your legacy and privacy. Loved ones aren't left lost, guessing at passwords or unable to claim what you built. With accounts mapped and tools in place, you're ready to document wishes for each digital asset and designate heirs or managers according to your values. This clarity makes the next phase of planning direct and manageable.

Creating a Comprehensive Digital Estate Plan

Building on your work cataloging digital assets, it's now time to turn that careful inventory into a detailed plan that secures your digital life for yourself and those you care about. Knowing exactly which bank accounts, cloud storage logins, social media profiles, and other online services you use gives you a strong foundation to decide what should happen to each one. Some accounts, like family email addresses or shared photo libraries, might hold sentimental value and need special handling. Others, such as investment platforms, business websites, or cryptocurrency wallets, could have financial consequences if left unmanaged or inaccessible. In chapter 10, we will discuss the legal landscape surrounding digital estates, privacy regulations, and the impact of platform terms of service on access to online accounts after death.

Start by documenting every asset on your list in a way that's clear and easy for someone else to understand. Use practical details for each: for a bank login, note not just the website address and username, but also how you currently access it (for example, via an authenticator app, saved phone number, or separate two-factor device). For photo libraries, list the cloud provider, the account email, and note if you've enabled automatic backups. Is it a personal account, for family, or business? Is it active, or has it gone unused for years? Write down which ones you check weekly, which sit dormant, and any you only use for work or gig jobs. If you aren't sure whether you still have access to an old account, or can't remember its password, set aside time to recover or delete it—this step will save your loved ones confusion later. If you run across accounts you forgot about, add them to your list and close any you no longer need.

For each item, include backup steps where needed, such as printing recovery codes for a password manager, storing seed words for a crypto wallet offline, or noting where two-factor authentication settings are kept. If your phone is essential for authentication, decide if it's labeled clearly somewhere. Keeping these details organized now keeps everything smoother for whoever steps in later, whether that's next month during a move, or years down the line when someone else needs to pick up the pieces.

As you review your inventory, think about who is best suited to inherit or shut down each kind of asset. The right digital steward often depends on the account type and what you want done with it. A sibling who works in IT might be perfect for handling encrypted files, while a friend who understands social media could help with memorial pages or removing private content. For investment apps or payment accounts, pick someone financially savvy who can follow proper closure steps and notify other stakeholders if needed. You might want different people for different jobs; that's fine. The main goal is that each digital asset has a clear, named person responsible and a written action: archive, delete, transfer, or just monitor.

Instructions should be specific: avoid saying “deal with my emails” and instead write, for example, “forward any emails from my accountant to my spouse, then close the account,” or “preserve my wedding photos in Google Photos and share access with my children.” A written list of wishes—rather than general requests—reduces the risk of loved ones guessing what you wanted or arguing about how something should be handled. Suppose you ran a personal blog for years, kept active social media accounts, and invested in stocks through a phone app. You may wish for your blog to be archived, your Facebook set to memorial, and your brokerage apps to be closed securely after the balance is settled. Each of these choices needs a contact name, access method, and clear instruction.

After deciding on heirs and actions, organize your directives as simply as possible. You can use a typed sheet, a handwritten page, an easy spreadsheet, or even a secure digital note, as long as the information is orderly: asset name, access steps, responsible contact, and intended action. Update these regularly; a good habit is to pick a recurring date—such as a birthday, tax time, or start of a new year—to review your documents and make changes. Store one digital copy in a secure cloud folder and print a version for your estate binder or safe deposit box so they're accessible even if your devices change.

Exercise — Build Your Digital Estate Plan

Prepare your own digital estate plan one step at a time. Break it into 20-minute sessions if it feels overwhelming.

1. Gather your asset list with account names and uses.
2. For each asset, add access details (login paths, devices used, backup codes if any).
3. Match each asset to a trusted contact and write a simple action (archive, delete, transfer).

4. Organize your notes: a spreadsheet, worksheet, or notebook.
5. Share the document's location with your designated digital heirs.
6. Set a calendar reminder to review this plan every 6–12 months.

Sample Entry:

- Asset: Gmail (Personal)
- Access: gmail.com, username, password manager, backup code in safe
- Contact: Angela (daughter)
- Action: Forward important messages to spouse, then close account

Follow these steps to give both yourself and your loved ones peace of mind about your digital life, knowing your wishes are clear, organized, and up to date.

Understanding Legal Considerations and Privacy Implications

When people finish recording their wishes and digital account details, they face a new challenge: navigating the maze of laws, privacy rules, and company policies that govern digital estate planning. It isn't enough to tell someone what you want done with your online accounts—legal restrictions and platform policies determine what an executor or loved one can actually do with digital assets.

Privacy and data protection laws set real limits. In the United States, the **Stored Communications Act (SCA)** restricts a service provider's ability to share email contents or private messages, even when there's a court order or written will. Companies like Google and Apple rely on this law to block unauthorized access, meaning heirs may be denied entry to cloud-based emails or drive files. In the

European Union, the **General Data Protection Regulation (GDPR)** imposes strict rules on personal data, often making it difficult for families to access accounts unless the original owner planned ahead. Many U.S. states have their own laws as well. For example, the **Revised Uniform Fiduciary Access to Digital Assets Act (RUFADAA)** grants executors or agents limited legal authority to manage digital assets—but only if explicit permission is given in legal documents.

Having a will or power of attorney doesn't guarantee access to everything online. When digital lives are tied to major platforms, their **terms of service** become the real gatekeepers. These contracts often state that accounts are licensed, not owned, allowing companies to restrict, suspend, or delete them at their discretion. For instance, Apple requires a court order and specific legal filings before releasing data from a deceased user's account, regardless of family wishes. Facebook lets users appoint a **Legacy Contact** to manage a memorialized profile but blocks access to private messages. Google's **Inactive Account Manager** allows a designated person to receive certain data after a set period of inactivity, but only for information the user marked as shareable. Executors who overlook these built-in tools may find themselves locked out, even with perfectly prepared legal documents.

Real-world cases reveal how powerful these digital barriers can be. Families have permanently lost years of shared photos when cloud storage companies refused access and no backup existed. In other cases, executors holding court orders, wills, and even passwords were still denied entry to a deceased person's email because company policy outweighed legal authority. When cryptocurrency wallets are involved, a missing password or seed phrase can erase entire fortunes—these assets often exist beyond the reach of both courts and estate law.

To reduce these risks and protect privacy, integrate safeguards directly into your digital estate plan. **Appoint a digital executor** and name that person in your legal documents to signal authorization to both courts and companies. This executor should know which accounts include legacy or inactive-manager tools and be ready to use them. When setting up features such as Google's Inactive Account Manager or Facebook's Legacy Contact, follow the platform's instructions precisely. Use two-factor authentication only where it won't interfere with access, and document where authentication keys or backup codes are stored. Never include passwords directly in wills or legal papers. Instead, store them securely in a **password manager**, and provide access instructions separately, in accordance with each service's policies.

Privacy does not end with death or incapacity. Someone's digital past—emails, messages, posts, and photos—can become public, misused, or lost if not handled with care. Imagine a scenario where an executor shares access too widely, and private family matters reach the wrong people. Or, where a law changes, and something once locked becomes open to others. Periodically review all plans, making sure account settings, privacy controls, and legal documents match current laws and platform rules. Most companies adjust service terms, privacy protections, and inheritance features over time. Ongoing checks are the only way to close gaps and stop surprises.

Laws and company rules will not always match personal wishes. Some assets—like certain online subscriptions or digital content—may not transfer at all under current laws. The safest path is making sure trusted people have legal authority, are trained in platform tools, and keep up with updates. Discussing these choices with loved ones and updating plans when laws or terms change provides peace of mind that your digital estate will be protected and respected the way you want.

Final Thoughts

Now that you understand the importance of managing and organizing your digital assets, you can take confident steps to protect your online presence for the future. By carefully documenting your accounts, setting up secure password management, and naming trusted contacts, you create a clear roadmap that guides your loved ones in carrying out your wishes with minimal stress and confusion. Staying informed about legal and privacy issues ensures your plan remains effective amid changing laws and platform rules. With an up-to-date digital estate plan in place, you safeguard not only financial assets but also cherished memories, providing peace of mind that your digital legacy will be respected and preserved.

CHAPTER 10

FAMILY CONVERSATIONS AND AVOIDING CONFLICT

"Why are we even talking about this now?" my sister asked, her voice tight with frustration. The room felt heavy as the words hung between us, an uncomfortable silence settling in afterward. I understood her hesitation—estate planning isn't easy to bring up, especially when emotions run high and relationships feel fragile. Yet avoiding the conversation doesn't erase the questions or concerns; it only leaves them simmering beneath the surface, ready to ignite at the worst possible time. These family talks are not just about dividing assets—they touch on trust, fairness, and the future of those we care about most. Facing them head-on takes courage, patience, and a clear approach that invites everyone in rather than shutting them out.

Communicating Your Plans and Involving Heirs Early

Some families delay estate planning discussions because they fear it will spark arguments, reopen old wounds, or stir uncomfortable emotions. Many adults worry that bringing it up will lead to hurt feelings or make it seem like they're planning for someone's absence too soon. Yet avoiding these talks often leads to silent misunderstandings, confusion, and conflict later—precisely when clarity is needed most. Open, honest conversations about estate plans give everyone a chance to understand, adjust, and contribute, preventing frustration and suspicion before they take root. Families who discuss these matters early and often often end up feeling more united and prepared, confident there won't be unpleasant surprises down the road.

Discussing estate planning is rarely easy, even among close families. Parents may dread their children questioning decisions about who inherits the house, the family business, or treasured keepsakes. Adult children, in turn, might fear appearing greedy or upsetting their parents by raising the topic at all. Beneath these worries usually lies a sincere desire to avoid pain, protect relationships, and ensure fairness for everyone involved.

What helps most is a clear, proactive approach that removes guesswork and invites participation. When everyone knows where they stand, they can plan together with confidence instead of speculating in silence. Including heirs and other key people early in the process makes a major difference. Once family members feel that decisions are being made behind closed doors, trust begins to erode—making any outcome feel unfair, even when it isn't. Early inclusion fosters shared purpose and reassurance instead of fear or resentment.

Consider a family who chooses to share their estate plans during a holiday gathering. Instead of waiting until someone asks or until a crisis forces the issue, the parents prepare a brief summary explaining how they want to divide property, what guided their choices, and which keepsakes hold special meaning. Each child has the opportunity to ask questions, share thoughts, or express interest in particular items. Everyone leaves the table feeling relieved, included, and more at peace about the future.

Practical Communication Tools for Estate Planning

Open communication takes intention and clear steps. Here are several practical strategies that help guide these sensitive discussions:

- **Schedule a dedicated family meeting** for estate planning, rather than mentioning it in passing. This signals respect for everyone's time and attention and sets aside a safe space for discussion.
- **Prepare a clear agenda** listing topics such as the will, trusts, healthcare decisions, and treasured possessions. Inform family members about the topic of discussion to avoid surprising them.
- **Explain your reasoning** for major decisions. For example, "We want the house to go to you because you have been living here and caring for it," or "We chose this executor because they understand financial matters."
- **Use plain language.** Avoid legal and financial jargon whenever possible, so no one feels left out or misunderstood.
- **Listen actively.** Give people time to share questions or worries without jumping in with answers or dismissing concerns.
- **Validate emotions.** If someone seems anxious or upset, acknowledge their feelings. Say, for instance, "I can see this makes you uncomfortable. Can you tell me what's concerning you?"
- **Invite honest feedback.** Encourage everyone to speak up if something doesn't feel right. This gives a chance to resolve tension early, rather than during a crisis later.

When a difficult topic arises—such as differing opinions about a family property or a child's worry about being left out—direct acknowledgment works best. If a child expresses fear that an inheritance will be unfair, the parent might say, "I understand why you're worried. Let's talk about how we came to this decision and see if we can address your concerns together." Including everyone's views shows respect and increases the sense of fairness.

Keeping the Conversation Going

One meeting is not always enough. Families grow, life circumstances change, and plans may need to be updated. Build trust further by establishing regular check-ins—perhaps once a year or after major events—to review plans, answer new questions, and share any adjustments. Keep written notes or a simple summary of each meeting, then distribute them to everyone. Documenting what was discussed and agreed on gives people peace of mind and reduces confusion.

Picture a family that gathers once every spring to revisit their estate plan. The parents share updates, invite questions, and give each child a copy of any changes. If a grandchild is born or someone's financial situation shifts, the family discusses how to reflect that in new arrangements.

Sometimes, openness does not prevent every disagreement. Some topics stay emotional, and resistance may surface anyway. Readers will need practical tools for addressing difficult reactions, which shapes the path forward for working through conflict and building lasting family trust.

Managing Resistance, Emotions, and Disagreements

Open and honest dialogue is more than a courtesy during estate planning—it builds the trust needed to navigate emotional reactions. When everyone feels heard and understood, even difficult conversations become easier to manage. Openness lays the groundwork for empathy, helping families face emotionally charged moments with clarity instead of frustration. For many adults, talking about inheritance, wills, or future care can stir strong feelings or surface old misunderstandings. These topics often touch deep insecurities, leading people to react defensively or withdraw. By focusing on clear and gentle communication, you create an atmosphere where emotional resistance has less power.

Estate planning conversations can trigger emotion for many reasons. Sibling rivalries may resurface when discussing how assets will be divided. One sibling might recall feeling overlooked or less favored, becoming more sensitive to perceived unfairness. Distrust can stem from old patterns—childhood conflicts over money or disagreements about how property was handled after a previous loss. Fear of being excluded is common, especially if adult children worry about their place in the family's future. Grief also plays a role, as reminders of aging or past losses can bring sadness close to the surface. Old resentments—about caregiving, support, or earlier disputes—can unexpectedly influence today's discussions. When families begin dividing property, memories of what mattered most often rise up, touching each person's sense of identity, belonging, or fairness.

Anger in these moments might sound like sharp words or heated arguments about what is "fair." Denial can appear as avoidance—refusing to engage, changing the subject, or insisting it's "too soon" to talk. Anxiety may show up through fidgeting, repeated questions, or indecision. Some people become defensive, interpreting questions as personal criticism. Others withdraw completely—falling silent or leaving the room to avoid pain. Imagine an adult son raising his voice as his parents explain their plans; he might feel his role in the family slipping away or believe his efforts are being overlooked. A daughter may grow quiet when her siblings discuss selling the family home if she associates that house with her childhood security.

There are reliable ways to navigate these challenging moments. The first is **active listening**—listening carefully, pausing before replying, and restating what you've heard to show understanding. For example: *"It sounds like you're worried about being left out of decisions. Is that right?"* This approach demonstrates that you value their feelings, even if you don't agree. When people feel understood, they often relax, opening the door to real conversation.

Staying calm under pressure is another skill worth developing. Practicing deliberate breathing—slow, steady breaths—can stop tension from escalating. Calling a brief time-out can also help; stepping away for a few minutes allows everyone to regain composure. For instance, if the discussion turns heated, you might say, *"Let's take a short break. I want to keep this conversation respectful."*

Framing difficult topics carefully reduces defensiveness. Begin with a clear purpose rather than blame or accusation. For example: *"My goal is to make sure everyone understands Dad's wishes so no one feels confused later."* Or, *"I want us all to feel this is as fair as possible."* Framing the conversation around shared understanding makes it easier for everyone to stay focused on solutions instead of feeling judged.

Defusing tension often means steering the conversation back to shared values or family goals. If an argument over asset division starts to boil, reminding everyone, "We all want to honor Mom's values and keep our family ties strong," can redirect focus. Grounding discussion in common reasons—the desire for fairness, clarity, and ongoing connection—eases the sense of competition or threat.

Recognizing emotional triggers helps families avoid missteps. Sometimes, simple misunderstandings become big problems. If one sibling feels accused when the discussion is only about process, clarifying intentions matters. For instance: "I'm not questioning your responsibility—I only want to make sure each person has input." Stating intentions openly can stop defensive reactions before they start.

Sometimes, strong feelings or repeated dead-ends signal the need for professional help. This can show up as the same fight erupting at every meeting or a family member raising past hurts that cannot be resolved in conversation. When this happens, mediators, family therapists, or neutral estate planning advisors can guide the group.

These professionals offer skills in managing conflict and keeping family discussions on track.

These tools empower you to manage family conversations with respect and effectiveness. By applying these techniques, you build not only agreement in the moment but also a strong foundation for future cooperation. When everyone understands the facts, intentions, and documents involved, future misunderstandings and conflicts become much easier to prevent—shaping a smoother path for estate planning and family harmony.

Creating Clarity to Prevent Future Conflicts

When families talk about estate planning, misunderstandings can cause lasting harm. Emotional topics sometimes lead to confusion or frustration, but a plan that spells out everything in plain words makes a real difference. Families find peace when no one has to guess what a loved one meant. That kind of certainty comes from clear, written instructions that leave nothing unsaid.

Some families discover this lesson through difficult experiences. Imagine siblings arguing after a parent's death because the will said, "split belongings equally," but did not list sentimental items. One child wants the family piano, another thinks it should go to whoever took care of it most, and everyone resents each other. Another family faces trouble when a parent's will names two people as guardians "if possible," with no other details. The uncertainty leads to arguments, legal bills, and hurt feelings that could last for years. Both families could have avoided these problems by spelling out their wishes in plain, detailed language and keeping clear, up-to-date records.

Clear estate planning starts with simple, direct words for every gift and request. Instead of saying, "Leave my jewelry to my children," list each piece and who should get it. Even small keepsakes cause big arguments when wishes are vague. If one child receives a treasured ring, explain in writing why you made this choice—maybe it was promised years ago, or it holds special meaning. Address things people may question. For example, if one child receives a larger share or a special gift, offer a note explaining your reasoning. Simple acts like this reduce hard feelings and give you a chance to share your values.

Ambiguity can also creep into the way people word gifts or divide assets. Avoid broad language like "as they see fit" or "to be shared fairly." Instead, specify either "my wedding album for my oldest daughter, Sarah Smith" or "the contents of my garage for my son, James Smith." Think about scenarios where things could go wrong. If you own a business, say exactly how you want it managed, sold, or handed down. Mention minority owners, outside partners, or key employees by name and say what will happen to their shares. Address the fate of second homes, vacation properties, or family land, including who will pay for upkeep and how you want the use decided.

There are steps that make sure your wishes remain clear and enforced. Keep all papers in an easy-to-find spot, like a fireproof box at home, or at your attorney's office. Here's how to manage your documents effectively:

Keep These Estate Planning Essentials

- Will (with clear, updated instructions)
- Trust documents (if set up)
- Letters of instruction for specific decisions
- List of assets and debts
- Copies of beneficiary forms for insurance and retirement accounts
- List of guardians, executors, trustees, and their contact details
- Power of attorney and medical directive paperwork
- List of professional contacts (attorney, accountant, insurance agent)times

After any big change—birth, marriage, divorce, or loss—look at your paperwork. Cross out the outdated details and write new instructions. If you moved, sold property, or made a major gift, make sure your plan matches your current situation.

Some areas almost always cause stress without guidelines. Blended families need extra care. If you want stepchildren to inherit, name them just as you do biological children. Avoid phrases like "all my children" unless you list everyone clearly. When it comes to family businesses, say who manages them, buys out shares, or receives profits—and what happens if there are disputes. For real estate, write what happens if someone wants to sell, but others do not. This prevents fights and court cases later.

- Some an unequal split is best for your family, but this can sting unless you explain your choice. Leave a letter behind that addresses your decisions in your own words. For example: "I am leaving my house to Sam because he cared for me and maintained the property. My other children receive extra cash to balance the gift."

People want to do the right thing, but they need guidance. Hold a family meeting before anything is final. Share your plan, tell your heirs where your records live, and let them ask questions. To keep the conversation positive, focus on why you made your choices, offer to answer concerns, and make it clear you want to avoid confusion. Sometimes these meetings feel tough, but they pay off by stopping arguments before they start.

Every important conversation, choice, or change should be written down and attached to your other papers. This means leaving a dated note whenever you update your wishes or talk about the estate plan with your family. These written records give your executors and heirs clear, strong proof of your intentions, so your voice remains steady and unmistakable even when you are gone.

Final Thoughts

Now that we understand the importance of open communication, managing emotions, and creating clear, detailed plans, we can approach estate planning with confidence and care. By involving family members early and speaking honestly, we build trust and reduce the chances of future disputes. Using practical tools to listen actively, address concerns gently, and document decisions clearly helps protect relationships and ensures everyone knows what to expect. With these strategies in place, you can create an estate plan that not only safeguards your assets but also strengthens your family's unity and peace of mind for years to come.

CHAPTER 11

KEEPING EVERYTHING ORGANIZED AND ACCESSIBLE

When a family suddenly faces the loss of a loved one, the last thing they need is confusion over important papers. Yet, all too often, critical documents like wills or powers of attorney are missing or hidden in unexpected places. One family spent weeks searching through offices and safety deposit boxes before finding a needed will tucked away in a forgotten briefcase. This delay added cost and deepened the stress during an already difficult time. Many people do not realize how easily such situations arise simply because estate plans are not kept in clear, accessible order. Without a reliable system for storing and sharing these documents, families can struggle to follow instructions or gain access when it matters most. These challenges highlight just how vital careful organization is to ensuring that your wishes are respected and that your loved ones are supported when you can no longer guide them yourself.

Storing Your Documents and Creating an Estate Binder

When life changes suddenly, families often find themselves searching for vital papers at the worst possible moments. One adult daughter recalled how, after her father's passing, no one could locate his original will. It took weeks of anxious searching and repeated trips to local banks before a copy finally turned up in an overlooked briefcase—causing costly legal delays and frayed nerves. This kind of confusion is entirely preventable. When records are organized, your instructions are easy to find and follow. Loved ones gain clarity, avoid guesswork, and spare themselves stress and unnecessary expense. Good organization becomes a quiet act of care—one that keeps chaos at bay when it matters most.

Strong organization begins with gathering every piece of your estate plan. Start by collecting the legal documents: your will, any trust agreements, power of attorney forms, and advance healthcare directives. Then add supporting materials such as insurance policies, property titles and deeds, beneficiary designation forms, bank and investment account details, and lists of passwords and key contacts. When everything sits together in one place, updates become simpler—and more importantly, those who must act on your behalf will have the information they need right away.

Begin assembling your **estate binder** by choosing a sturdy, spacious binder or legacy folder—something durable enough to protect the contents and easy to handle. Add wide dividers or color-coded tabs to separate each section for quick reference. Consider the following divisions:

- Legal Documents (will, trusts, powers of attorney)
- Financial Accounts (bank statements, investment notes)
- Beneficiary Forms and Insurance Policies
- Medical Information (advance directives, Do Not Resuscitate orders)
- Property Records (house deeds, car titles)
- Key Contacts (lawyer, accountant, financial advisor, family names and numbers)
- Personal Instructions (letters to family, digital account information, passwords)

Slip a simple checklist or table of contents at the front. This page offers a snapshot of what's inside and eases the process of checking for missing paperwork when you update things down the road.

Choose a home for your binder that balances safety with accessibility. A locked filing cabinet, fireproof safe, or secure drawer works well. Avoid bank safe deposit boxes—families often struggle to access them at critical moments if the account holder isn't present. Pick a location that's protected from water or fire, yet easy enough for trusted people to find when needed.

Physical folders are only half the story. Back up your estate plan with **digital copies** to protect against loss or damage. Begin by scanning signed, finalized versions of every important document. Many home printers have built-in scanners, or you can use free phone apps for this task. Save the files on an external hard drive or a secure, encrypted cloud service. Cloud platforms such as Google Drive, Dropbox, or OneDrive work well—just make sure to enable **two-factor authentication** for added protection.

When naming your digital files, keep labels simple and consistent—for example, *LastWill_JohnSmith_2024.pdf* or *POA_MarySmith_2023.pdf.* Create main folders that match the sections of your physical binder: **Legal, Finance, Insurance, Health, Property, Contacts,** and **Personal.** Avoid generic file names or dumping everything into one folder. Clear, logical organization saves time and prevents confusion when someone else needs to locate documents quickly.

Always password-protect any folders or drives containing sensitive files. Consider using a password manager to store combinations securely and share access with only the most trusted individuals. Besides storing in the cloud, keep a backup copy on a separate, encrypted external drive. If the house suffers a disaster, digital backups can ensure nothing gets lost. Periodically check your backups to make certain everything works properly and stays up to date.

Sensitive papers need both protection from outsiders and immediate access for loved ones in case of an emergency. Avoid hiding document binders or encrypted files so well that even responsible family members cannot locate them under pressure. For the physical binder, show at least one trusted person where it is and how to open any locks. For digital storage, share clear written instructions (and necessary passwords) either in person, in a sealed envelope, or through your attorney.

A thoughtful organization method means you do more than gather papers—you set family members up to succeed when the time comes. Passing along the secret location of your binder, a shared drive, or handoff instructions gives those you trust the real gift: the ability to act swiftly on your behalf, without stumbling through guesswork. Ensuring access is the natural next step to making your organizational efforts truly helpful and lasting.

Sharing Access with Key People

A carefully organized folder, binder, or digital file only provides real protection for your loved ones if people know exactly where to find these documents. Many families keep their will, power of attorney, or healthcare directives locked away, only to discover in a crisis that nobody knows the location or how to access them. When you organize your estate documents, the next step is thinking about who will need to find them quickly in times of illness, incapacity, or after your passing.

Imagine a scenario where an adult child needs a parent's will to start probate but cannot even find the right drawer. Or a power of attorney document sits encrypted on a laptop, with the password long forgotten. This happens more often than many expect, leading to expensive legal delays, locked bank accounts, or confusion at the hospital. Families left without guidance often feel lost and sometimes need a court's permission to take basic steps. On the other hand, when people receive clear directions—such as a spouse shown exactly where documents are and how to access digital files—they resolve matters quickly and privately.

Being selective about who can find and use your estate planning documents keeps your information safe while ensuring someone trustworthy is always prepared. Most people choose a spouse, adult child, or executor. Others involve a trusted friend or financial advisor. The important thing is not to give everyone access but to think through who genuinely needs it. This keeps your plan private, shields your documents from outsiders, and protects your legacy from unnecessary eyes.

Start by making a short, clear list of the individuals who should know about your estate documents. Consider their reliability, location, and your comfort level. Then, decide the best way to share information securely.

Ways to Communicate Document Locations

Face-to-Face Conversation

- Invite the person to a private space.
- Explain what documents you have and where you store them.
- If there are keys or combination codes involved, show them how to access these.
- Walk through the process together if possible.

Written Instructions

- Write a simple, clear note outlining each document's name and storage location.
- List any steps needed (for example, "key to box is in kitchen drawer").

- Place this note in a secure spot, such as a safe deposit box or family safe.
- Tell your trusted individual how to find the note.

Family or Executor Meeting

- Gather only those who genuinely need this information.
- Share general details—what exists and who can access it—without revealing passwords or private legal details in front of everyone.
- Allow time for questions so there is no remaining uncertainty.

Sharing Digital Access Safely

Digital asset management is more common with wills or financial documents stored on computers or in cloud folders. The risk comes if a password, security question, or device lockout keeps your team from retrieving what's needed.

- Keep a password list in a locked safe or safe deposit box. Update it when you change passwords.
- Use a password management tool with shared access features. Many offer the ability to add a trusted emergency contact.
- Prepare sealed envelopes containing access instructions to be given to your attorney or executor. The envelope stays shut until needed.
- Never email passwords or sensitive information, as messages can be intercepted or accounts hacked.

Example of a Clear Password Sharing Process

1. Write or print a list of passwords for all devices and key accounts.
2. Place the list in a sealed envelope.
3. Store the envelope in a fireproof safe.
4. Give your chosen person instructions on where to find the envelope and when to use it.
5. Check every six to twelve months that the passwords are still current.

Protecting Privacy and Security

Share information only through safe, controlled means. Refrain from sending storage details by text or email. Communicate sensitive details only by secure phone call, trusted written note, or in person.

Make it easy for your trusted helper to report changes, lost keys, or a forgotten password. Whenever you move documents or update passwords, let the right people know as soon as possible. Schedule check-ins or short meetings if circumstances change or a review feels necessary. Encourage your helpers to ask questions if they are unclear what steps to take.

Written instructions offer reassurance that no step will be forgotten. Keep them simple, and make sure they are available when needed. At the same time, store them where only the appropriate person can access them to avoid theft or tampering.

Building a routine for sharing updates and open communication with your trusted contacts means your estate plan will stay accurate as your life changes. Regular touchpoints with your key people make it much easier to keep everything up to date, supporting the full intent behind your careful organization. This clear chain of access equips your family with confidence, saves time, and reduces legal headaches when the unexpected occurs.

Setting Calendar Reminders for Regular Updates

Staying on top of estate planning requires more than building trust and sharing information with loved ones. Even after decisions are made and documents are in order, estate planning should be treated as an ongoing responsibility. Life continually evolves—new family members arrive, finances shift, and health circumstances change. Without regular reviews and timely updates, an estate plan can easily fall out of step with reality. Outdated information or overlooked details may lead to confusion, legal delays, and extra costs at the very moment when clarity matters most. Loved ones may struggle to carry out your wishes if they aren't clearly or fully expressed.

Regular review is the best way to keep an estate plan current and effective. Scheduling a yearly check-in helps everything stay organized and up to date. Tying your review to a familiar annual milestone works well—many people choose tax season, the start of summer, a birthday, or the beginning of the school year. Linking the task to a recurring event turns it into a habit rather than a chore. For example, you might decide to revisit your estate plan each spring after filing taxes. This approach keeps the process simple, structured, and less likely to be forgotten.

Sudden life events can also signal the need for immediate updates. After a marriage, divorce, the birth of a child or grandchild, a major purchase such as a new home, a significant health change, or the loss of a loved one, take time to ensure your plan still reflects your current reality. Here are some examples to keep in mind:

- Getting married or divorced can mean changing or adding beneficiaries.
- Having a baby or grandchild might call for an update to the will or trust.
- Moving to a new home means updating property records and addresses.

- Opening or closing accounts requires checking that ownership and beneficiaries are current.
- Serious health changes may prompt you to revisit powers of attorney or healthcare directives.

To make these good intentions stick, reminders are crucial. Digital calendars make it easy to set recurring annual alerts. In Google Calendar or Outlook, add a new event for "Estate Plan Review," set the date to your chosen milestone, and select "repeat yearly." Set a phone alarm for the same day to have an extra nudge. If you prefer physical reminders, write the review date on a family wall calendar or your planner. Marking the date in a visible spot puts the task front and center—as likely to be noticed as any family birthday. People less comfortable with digital tools can follow these simple steps:

1. Pick a regular event or fixed date (for example, April 15).
2. On a smartphone, open the calendar app and tap the date.
3. Add an event titled "Estate Plan Review."
4. Set the event to repeat each year.
5. Select a notification alert—many phones let you get a reminder a day ahead.
6. Also, write the date on your home calendar or planner for backup.

Alongside reminders, a quick checklist for maintaining an estate plan can bring order to the process. Place this checklist right inside your estate planning folder or save it in the same digital location as your documents. A typical checklist might look like this:

- Check beneficiary designations for all life insurance, retirement, and investment accounts
- Review will instructions and asset lists
- Confirm powers of attorney for finances and healthcare reflect current wishes
- Update healthcare directives as needed

- Review account titles and ownership for new or closed accounts
- Confirm contact lists for lawyers, financial advisors, and emergency contacts are up-to-date

Reviewing these items annually ensures accuracy and readiness for future requirements.

Documenting each review and change is valuable for both clarity and peace of mind. On the first page of each estate document, write the review date by hand or add a note to the digital file. For major changes, keep a short change log or summary sheet in the same folder, listing the date and reason for each update. For example, write: "June 5, 2024—Changed primary residence address after moving." Keeping these notes makes it easy for family or professionals to follow your decisions and understand your intentions.

A well-maintained estate plan serves as a steady safety net for family and friends. It protects not only property but also relationships, avoiding conflict and confusion during already stressful times. Taking just a little time each year to review, update, and record changes creates lasting reassurance that your wishes will be understood and honored when the time comes.

Bringing It All Together

Now that you understand the importance of organizing, storing, sharing, and regularly updating your estate planning documents, you can take confident steps to secure your family's future. By creating an accessible estate binder, backing up digital copies, and clearly communicating access with trusted individuals, you reduce confusion and costly delays when your plan is needed most. Setting calendar reminders for annual reviews and promptly updating changes ensures your wishes remain current and clear over time. This careful preparation protects your assets and provides peace of mind, knowing your loved ones have the guidance they need to carry out your intentions smoothly and without unnecessary stress.

CHAPTER 12

UPDATING YOUR ESTATE PLAN AS LIFE CHANGES

Have you ever made an important plan, only to have life change in ways you didn't expect? Maybe you got married, had a child, or experienced a shift in your finances. How confident are you that the plan you created still fits your current situation? Many people put time into making an estate plan, but few realize how often it needs to be reviewed and updated. What happens if you forget to adjust your wishes after significant changes occur? Could outdated documents cause confusion or unintended consequences for those you care about most? These are common concerns that many face but seldom prepare for. Understanding when and why to revisit your estate plan is key to making sure it accurately reflects your life today —and the future you want to protect.

Key Moments to Update and Edit Your Estate Plan

Significant changes in life often mean it is time to look over your estate plan. Careful updates make sure your wishes are clearly carried out and your loved ones are protected. Missing a review can create confusion, legal trouble, and heartbreak in times that are already stressful. Many people don't realize just how many types of events can affect an estate plan's integrity.

Marriage or Divorce

Marriage typically means you want your spouse to be taken care of. If your will or beneficiary forms don't mention your new spouse, they might not inherit anything directly, or an ex-spouse could remain the main beneficiary. This situation becomes more complicated in blended families with children from previous relationships. During a divorce, if you forget to remove your former spouse from documents, they might still receive life insurance benefits, act as your healthcare agent, or inherit everything you leave behind.

Real-world example

Imagine someone names their spouse as the sole beneficiary of their retirement account. Years later, they divorce, but never update the beneficiary. If that person dies, the ex-spouse may still receive the full account, even if the person has remarried. Courts often uphold the named beneficiary, regardless of personal wishes or the current marriage.

New Children and Changing Family Structures

When a child is born or adopted, a review is in order. If you do not add the new child or update guardianship appointments, that child could be left with nothing or be without a clear guardian if both parents pass away. Families also shift when adult children become old enough to take on responsibilities. They may need to be added as agents for power of attorney or trusted representatives in case you're unable to make your own decisions.

What Can Go Wrong

Suppose your will was drafted before your youngest child was born. If nothing changes, only your older children may inherit, while your youngest is left out. Or maybe you have health care directives that name your brother as your agent, but now your adult daughter is better suited for the job.

Significant Changes in Financial Status

Financial ups and downs matter too. Inheriting a large sum, getting a major job bonus, or selling a business can all reshape your plan. If these gains and losses aren't reflected in your instructions, your plan might not divide wealth as you want. Taxes on inheritance or gifts given during life can also be different, so updating may help your family avoid big bills.

Example

If your estate plan was built around a house and modest savings, but then you launch a successful business, that business needs to be considered. Mishandling business succession can trigger family arguments, or tax headaches that drain the value of your hard work.

Becoming a Caregiver or Needing Care

Taking care of aging parents, or if you develop health concerns, means plans should list divorce but your bank accounts or health decisions. Appointing powers of attorney or updating advance directives lets people step in at the right time with the legal authority to make choices. If too many documents exist with different names, or if outdated forms forget new helpers, it can cause power struggles or gaps in care.

The Risks of Not Making Official, Legal Updates

Handwritten changes in the margins, crossing out names, or making promises aloud aren't enough. These attempts often get challenged and usually fail in court. Each state has rules about signatures, witnesses, and what makes a document valid. Skipping any step can mean your plan isn't followed, period.

Working with Professionals

Even if you use an online service to fill out forms, it's smart to check with an estate planning attorney. They double-check that everything fits together, follows current laws, and closes any loopholes. A professional also spots issues like outdated beneficiary forms for retirement accounts or insurance policies, which aren't controlled by your will or trust. These forms need their own review and updates, or old choices can override your intentions.

Staying Organized and Proactive

Set annual or biannual reminders to review your full set of documents. Create a checklist for each life event:

- Will and trusts
- Beneficiary designations for retirement, investment, and insurance accounts
- Power of attorney and health care directives
- Guardianship nominations

Compare each form to your real-life relationships and finances. Make sure every name, amount, and responsibility is accurate, with no old contacts left over.

What Happens When Updates Are Neglected

Skipping a review can mean a special needs child is left without support, or adult children fight in court over medical decisions. Loved ones might have to endure drawn-out probate battles, or face large taxes that could have been avoided.

Life keeps moving, but laws and technology around estate planning change too. Being alert to these shifts means your wishes stay current and safe regardless of future developments.

Adapting to Legal and Technological Changes

Estate planning requires close attention when major life events call for quick action—but those moments are only part of the bigger picture. Life keeps moving, and so do the laws and tools that shape how an estate plan functions in practice. Keeping everything up to date means staying alert to legal changes and new strategies that might alter what's possible—or even disrupt arrangements you put in place years ago. The plans designed to protect your family's future need ongoing care, not just a one-time signature.

Estate laws can change at both the federal and state levels, sometimes in ways that surprise even experienced planners. After a marriage, divorce, the birth of a child, or a financial shift, it's natural to update your documents. But what happens when Congress lowers the federal estate tax exemption? If the amount of wealth you can pass on tax-free decreases, your plan might unintentionally expose heirs to new taxes. State governments also adjust regulations for items like health care directives and powers of attorney. A document that was valid three years ago might no longer meet current standards. For instance, if your state tightens the signing requirements for a living will, your document could be ruled invalid—and your wishes ignored as a result.

The details of beneficiary designations also come under scrutiny in changing legal environments. Sometimes, rules about who can inherit retirement accounts shift, or states introduce new forms for registering transfer-on-death designations. If you're not watching these changes, you could unintentionally disinherit a loved one or make the asset transfer process longer and costlier for your family.

The most powerful step in staying current is to take an active role in monitoring legal developments that affect estate planning. Reliable information can be found through official state government websites and the Internal Revenue Service for federal tax laws. Estate planning organizations often produce plain-language updates about changes in statutes or case law. Many attorneys' offices issue timely legal bulletins or offer summaries following major policy updates. Monitoring these sources can assist you in identifying significant changes that could impact your plan.

Professional help adds another layer of security and comfort. Law and policy updates can be confusing, which makes regular contact with an estate planning attorney or financial advisor very helpful. Scheduling an annual or biannual document review takes only a small amount of time, and in return, you receive peace of mind that your plan remains effective and legally sound. Some professionals offer email newsletters; subscribing connects you to timely alerts about the latest developments. Examples include your attorney reviewing your trust after state tax laws shift or your advisor helping you see what new retirement account rules mean for your intended heirs. These relationships offer both day-to-day support and deep guidance when large-scale legal changes occur.

Technology brings welcome simplicity and speed to estate planning. New tools can help you keep your documents secure, up-to-date, and easily accessible to those who need them. Secure online document vaults store digital copies of your most important paperwork, from wills to powers of attorney, and let you grant access to trusted family members or advisors. Encryption keeps your sensitive information safe, while cloud storage makes it possible to update forms without waiting for meetings or mailing paperwork.

Asset inventory apps let you record valuables, accounts, and digital assets—all in one place.

Online platforms simplify communication with professionals and loved ones. Instead of mailing forms or scheduling in-person signings each time there's a small change, you can use digital signature tools or secure portals to share updates fast. With more wealth held in digital accounts and even cryptocurrencies, planning for so-called "digital assets" has become vital. Having a clear process for passing on email, financial accounts, or cryptocurrency keys prevents loss and confusion for your heirs.

Some actionable steps help keep your estate plan on track in a changing world:

- Keep a recurring checklist to review plan documents in light of new legal or tax conditions each year.
- Organize your estate documents in both digital and paper versions, storing each securely and keeping track of who has access.
- Sign up for legal update emails from attorneys, estate planning organizations, and trusted financial sources.
- Use online portals or secure messaging to communicate changes with multiple professionals at once.
- After tax law changes, update your will or trust as soon as possible, even if you only need to adjust a few details.

Staying alert and making use of professional advice, supported by good digital tools, is the simplest way to keep your plan effective into the future. Active care protects your loved ones from surprises and hassle. Establishing the habit of reviewing, discussing, and refining your plans regularly turns estate management into a protective tradition that can support your family across generations.

Making Estate Planning a Lifelong Habit

After looking at the big forces—like changing laws and evolving technology—that can affect estate planning, it becomes clear that building regular review habits matters just as much. Treating estate planning as a single event feels natural in the beginning. People check the boxes, sign the documents, and set them aside. Later, this can cause trouble for families who realize too late that things have drifted out of date. Over time, it is quiet, steady attention that preserves both intentions and peace of mind.

Small steps done every year take less effort than major overhauls, and they help the plan stay reliable as life changes. One simple trick is to put an annual reminder on a phone or digital calendar. This prompt gives a nudge to pull out estate documents and double-check important details. Instead of feeling overwhelmed, readers can set aside just an afternoon to look over beneficiary designations, will instructions, or any healthcare directives. Digital tools, like reminder apps and calendar scheduling, make this habit almost automatic. Someone who receives an alert every January will remember to look for errors, outgrown appointments, or family changes reflected in their paperwork.

Pairing this annual review with a personal milestone can help it feel more natural instead of forced. Marking birthdays, anniversaries, or even tax season as moments to glance at estate materials gives the routine a built-in cue. For example, one family decided that each year during tax filing, they would also check that their children's guardianship arrangements and account lists were still right. Another person set up a calendar invite for her birthday so she could look over her documents while also celebrating how much had changed in her life since the previous year. For many, these seasonal reminders keep the topic from becoming forgotten or overwhelming.

Estate planning is not just about paperwork—it's about people. Encouraging open communication within the family makes a meaningful difference. Holding regular family meetings, even once a year, helps everyone stay aligned on wishes, roles, and expectations. It's best to keep these conversations structured but simple. Topics might include reviewing account changes, welcoming new family members through marriage or birth, or noting any health concerns.

Starting these discussions can feel uncomfortable at first. Some families find it easier to begin with gratitude—saying something like, *"I want to thank everyone for helping make sure our plans stay current."* Others break the ice by referencing a real-life example, such as a news story about estate confusion after someone's passing. Using outside examples or appreciation can help shift the tone from tense to cooperative.

Sharing responsibility among family members also strengthens the process. Instead of one person managing everything, divide tasks so each person handles a specific part—like tracking health updates, keeping a digital asset list, or maintaining a secure folder of documents. One family found success by assigning one member to oversee health records, another to organize account passwords, and a third to maintain the estate binder. With each person holding a manageable piece, no one feels overwhelmed, and important details receive consistent attention. Delegating in this way builds trust and ensures that essential knowledge isn't lost if someone becomes unavailable.

Keeping a clear, updated **checklist** brings order to even the most complicated life changes. Beyond wills and powers of attorney, include digital assets such as email accounts, cloud storage, social media logins, streaming services, and even phone passcodes. If no one can find these details when needed, frustration and wasted time often follow. For instance, one widow spent weeks trying to access her late husband's email, only to discover the password had been discarded with a sticky note. Another family used a shared password manager, keeping every update in sync—making transitions simple and stress-free for everyone involved.

A proactive approach to estate planning offers quiet benefits that surface during life's most challenging times. Relatives feel less stress when they already know where to look and whom to ask for information. Family members understand their responsibilities, wishes get carried out more clearly, and even small moments of reflection reinforce bonds. An up-to-date plan helps prevent fights or confusion, which often come from surprises hidden in old paperwork.

Routine review of an estate plan deserves a spot alongside annual finances and health checkups. This is not only about paperwork or savings but also about family stability and peace of mind. Turning maintenance into a habit means that loved ones will face fewer obstacles, smoother transitions, and a lasting legacy that really fits readers' true wishes. Making the time each year to review and communicate provides everyone a stronger sense of security—something that no single, one-time effort can provide.

Concluding Thoughts

Now that we understand the many life changes and legal shifts that can impact an estate plan, it is clear that regular updates are not optional but essential. By making a habit of reviewing and adjusting your documents annually or after major events, you ensure your wishes remain accurate and legally sound. This ongoing attentiveness protects your family from confusion, costly disputes, and unexpected tax burdens. Embracing a proactive approach, with help from professionals when needed, turns estate planning into a manageable routine that secures your legacy and provides lasting peace of mind for you and those you care about most.

YOUR VOICE CAN PROTECT SOMEONE'S LEGACY

Every plan we create today can become a **gift of clarity** for someone tomorrow.

Have you thought about what would happen to your family if you weren't there to help?

Picture a grieving family—already overwhelmed—trying to navigate courts, paperwork, and financial confusion because no clear estate plan was left behind. Your reflections on ***Estate Planning*** could give future readers the reassurance and direction they need to avoid this painful scenario.

If this book helped you *understand the essentials*, *organize your assets more clearly*, or *take the first steps toward protecting your family*, I'd be truly honored if you would leave a short, honest review.

Your feedback not only supports my work—it also becomes a **beacon** for readers who may be standing right where you once stood: *uncertain, hesitant, but ready to protect what matters most.* Even a few sentences can ripple outward, helping others find the tools and courage to prepare for their future.

Thank you for reading, reflecting, and sharing your journey. **Your words carry more power than you may realize.**

CONCLUSION

You've taken important steps on a journey that, for many people, feels overwhelming before it even begins. By creating an estate plan—one tailored to your life and the people you love—you've not only secured peace of mind for yourself but also provided protection and clarity for those dearest to you. The confidence that comes from knowing your wishes are clear and your future provisions are in place is no small accomplishment. As you reach the end of this process, recognize the gift you've created: stability, certainty, and care, all delivered with intention and love.

Throughout this book, we explored the key components of an effective estate plan, breaking down what often feels complicated into manageable, actionable steps. We began by showing that estate planning isn't only for the wealthy or the elderly—it's a practical act of care for anyone who has assets, responsibilities, or loved ones they wish to protect. Whether you're in your thirties and beginning to build wealth, a parent focused on your children's security, a homeowner hoping to avoid probate delays, or someone caring for aging relatives, your circumstances make estate planning both relevant and necessary.

At the heart of every estate plan are the core documents that form its foundation. A **will** ensures that your property and belongings are distributed according to your wishes, preventing confusion and disputes among family members. **Powers of attorney**—for both finances and healthcare—place trusted individuals in charge if you ever become unable to make decisions yourself. **Health care directives** outline the treatments you want or wish to avoid, sparing loved ones from making painful choices in emotional moments. **Living trusts** can provide privacy, shorten probate, and reduce the risk of legal challenges. When these documents are clear, current, and well organized, they can turn what might be a stressful transition into a smooth and confident one for your family.

Equally important are the decisions you've already started making throughout this process. You identified who you trust to carry out your wishes, thoughtfully considered guardianship for your children or dependents, and clarified your intentions regarding health care and financial matters. For homeowners, you assessed how your property would transfer, possibly avoiding lengthy court proceedings. If you have special accounts, insurance policies, or retirement plans, you updated beneficiaries so everything aligns seamlessly. Each choice was a step toward relieving future burdens and ensuring your legacy is preserved with integrity.

Many readers begin this book feeling unsure where to start or anxious about making mistakes. That's understandable. Legal language can be intimidating, and the thought of sitting down to consider end-of-life scenarios is rarely appealing. But you have seen that planning is not an all-or-nothing task. Each piece fits together over time, at your pace. Remember, perfection is not required—progress is what truly matters. Even imperfect plans, updated as your life evolves, make an enormous difference compared to having no plan at all.

If you ever find yourself hesitating, remember that estate planning is a living process. You can begin today by putting just one document in place—even something as simple as drafting a basic will or naming a power of attorney. As life evolves, revisit your plan periodically. Adjustments are not only natural, they're wise. Milestones such as marriage, divorce, the birth of a child, or changes in your financial situation all call for thoughtful updates. No matter your age or stage in life, now is always the right time to begin.

It's also natural to have questions or face unique circumstances. Seeking guidance is a sign of strength, not uncertainty. Many people choose to consult a qualified attorney for complex estates, blended families, business ownership, or other special considerations. With today's wide range of online tools and affordable planning software, you can also begin the process independently—reviewing drafts and options at your own pace before deciding whether professional input is needed. Whichever path you choose, include your family in the conversation. Open communication prevents misunderstanding and reinforces the true purpose of your planning: to care for the people you love.

Leaving a legacy isn't defined by the size of your bank account or the number of properties you own. It's about preserving your values, protecting those closest to you, and minimizing unnecessary cost and stress. Estate planning gives your family the freedom to focus on healing and supporting one another instead of struggling through confusion and paperwork. The stories you share, the memories you pass on, and the thoughtful instructions you leave behind are among the most meaningful gifts you can offer.

Consider the peace that comes from having a plan in hand. Your loved ones are spared guesswork. Vital information is accessible when needed most. Bills get paid, homes are protected, and cherished possessions find their way to the people who will value them most. With the steps you have taken—and those you continue to take—you affirm that your wishes matter and that those who count on you will be cared for, no matter what. This is your legacy, shaped by your decisions and grounded in your intention.

It's natural to still wonder if you've done enough or if your plan will stand the test of time. Rest assured, the effort you have invested will make a lasting impact. While laws may change and your life may shift; foundational steps—updating documents, communicating wishes, and selecting trustworthy representatives—will always be relevant. Regular reviews ensure that your plan remains current. Most importantly, your loved ones will understand that they were your top priority at every stage.

Now is the moment to celebrate both the clarity you've created and the empowerment you feel. You haven't just checked off a legal requirement; you've claimed control over your future and given your family a roadmap for navigating life's transitions. Let this accomplishment spur you forward. If there are still pieces left unfinished, return to them with renewed confidence. If you're ready to take the next step, reach out for expert help or leverage technology to fine-tune your plan. If the hardest part—a conversation about the future—awaits, open the dialogue with honesty and care.

Take pride in what you've achieved. You've built something priceless: a safety net for those you love most, designed on your terms. Every page turned, every decision made, has moved you closer to lasting peace of mind. Let this mark the beginning—not the end—of living with greater assurance, knowing your legacy will endure through whatever tomorrow may bring.

www.ingramcontent.com/pod-product-compliance
Lightning Source LLC
Chambersburg PA
CBHW050528240926
51846CB00003B/743
* 9 7 8 1 9 7 0 8 3 9 0 7 4 *